RETURN
—— *of the* ——
EXILED CHILD

A Mindful Journey from Trauma
to Wholeness

BY
KEITH W. FIVESON

Praise for the Book

Dr. Anna Yusim, M.D.

Clinical Assistant Professor, Yale School of Medicine; Author of Fulfilled: How the Science of Spirituality Can Help You Live a Happier, More Meaningful Life

In a world that prizes productivity over presence and performance over peace, *Return of the Exiled Child* is not just a book – it's a homecoming. Keith Fiveson has done something rare: he has woven clinical wisdom, spiritual depth, and raw human vulnerability into a tapestry that doesn't just describe healing; it invites it. Drawing from Internal Family Systems, mindfulness, and his own courageous journey, Keith illuminates the hidden architecture of our inner world – the protectors, the exiles, the silent child curled in the closet of our psyche – and shows us how to return to them not as broken fragments, but as sacred parts of a whole self waiting to be reclaimed.

As a psychiatrist who sits with high-achieving, trauma-adapted individuals every day – CEOs, artists, and athletes – I see the cost of exile: burnout masked as success, numbness mistaken for strength, and relational patterns replaying childhood wounds. This book offers an antidote: not through fixing, but through fierce, tender presence.

Return of the Exiled Child doesn't ask you to transcend your pain. It asks you to sit with it. To breathe with it. To whisper, "I'm here now." And in that simple act, to stitch your soul back together.

If you've ever felt split between who you are and who you had to become to survive, read this book – not as a manual, but as a mirror. Because the child you left behind is still waiting, and Keith Fiveson hands you the lantern to find your way back.

Stephanie Campbell, M.S.W.

Senior Vice President, Kent Strategic Advisors; Adjunct Professor, NYU Silver School of Social Work

It's a rare gift to find a book that functions not only as a map for recovery but also as a heartfelt reflection of a life courageously lived and gently reclaimed. *Return of the Exiled Child* does this beautifully. Thank you for offering us more than just a memoir or process – you share your medicine bundle on how to heal from the intergenerational bundle passed from one generation to the next: a path of healing that blends Internal Family Systems, Adult Children of Alcoholics principles, and embodied mindfulness.

You bring to life the inner dramas and survival strategies so many of us inherit, showing how we can return with presence, tenderness, and radical acceptance. For those from families affected by alcoholism and trauma, this story offers permission to move beyond survival toward chosen belonging. The insights on dreamwork, breath, and the somatic act of return feel not only therapeutic but ceremonial, reminding us that healing is not a destination but a rhythm, a way of living.

Most of all, I am grateful for the humility and hope that inspire this work. You do not preach but sit beside us. You do not prescribe but show us what's needed and how to map the restoration of sanity.

Your work leaves us feeling less alone, more whole, and able to honor our own Golden Child - not with the burden of perfection, but with the grace of presence.

Dr. Alexander Shester, M.D.
Psychiatrist and Jungian Analyst

As a psychiatrist and Jungian Analyst, I have treated many who suffered severe childhood trauma. *Return of the Exiled Child* stands out as an extraordinary account of transformation: a profound journey from trauma and illness to the emergence of wisdom and wholeness.

The book's power lies in its rare blend of memoir and practical guidance. Fiveson shares his painful experiences with humility and vulnerability, demonstrating how a shattered psyche can heal and integrate. Drawing on Internal Family Systems and Jungian archetypes, he personifies aspects of the psyche – once protective mechanisms – and transforms them into guides on the journey from Exiled Child to Inner Golden Child.

He weaves psychology, spirituality, and transpersonal insight with mindfulness, breathwork, and emerging trauma therapies. Beautiful artwork and exercises deepen engagement. Lyrical and wise, *Return of the Exiled Child* is among the most creative works on psychological healing I've read. It serves both as moving narrative and valuable guide for psychotherapists, healers, and seekers alike.

Dr. Kristin Barnes, N.D., EAMP
Naturopathic Doctor & Eastern Asian Medicine Practitioner

I was not prepared for the depth of this book. Its rawness startled me, because I felt like I was seeing myself in these pages. The work is a marvelous acknowledgment of how complex humans and their relationships are. I loved the idea of "internal feng shui" – arranging our interior life with the same intention we bring to sacred spaces.

Certain lines stayed with me:

"Some transformations unfold quietly, in spaces where nothing seems to be happening." "While these environments looked elegant on the surface, they often exacted a toll." "The digital world didn't cause the disconnection, it revealed it."

This book invites stillness and wholeness. The answer isn't a grand epiphany – it's the quiet realization that healing is simply being.

Dr. Randall S. Hansen, Ph.D.
Founder, EmpoweringSites.com; Author & Educator

A powerful book that invites readers on a journey of self-discovery and healing. It explains and demonstrates the need and power of healing while guiding us through deep reflection, archetypal awareness, and stories from the author's own life. Drawing on Internal Family Systems, breathwork, and somatics, Fiveson shows that we can move toward a better, happier, and healed life. Healing is not the finish line; it's the beginning of truly being you.

Judson Davis, Ph.D.
Jungian Psychologist & Scholar of Consciousness Studies

Return of the Exiled Child draws on both Eastern and Western traditions to illuminate healing and integration. Through five universal pathways and archetypal figures, Fiveson offers a psychologically sound guide for the journey from the Exiled Child to the Golden Child – a return to wholeness uniting body and spirit.

Catherine Maudsley
Art Historian & Educator

Visually evocative and spiritually resonant, Keith's work captures what words alone cannot – the subtle light of transformation. His synthesis of art, psychology, and mindfulness offers a window into the heart of human resilience.

Matt Zemon DMin, MSc,
Author of The Beginner's Guide to Psychedelics.

For years I have sat with people in ceremony as they meet parts of themselves they exiled long ago. Sometimes that reunion is gentle. Sometimes it is not. Keith Fiveson has written the map for that return. Return of the Exiled Child belongs in the hands of every seeker preparing to sit with sacred medicine, and every guide helping them integrate what they found.

Return of the Exiled Child
A Mindful Journey from Trauma to Wholeness

© 2025 Keith W. Fiveson

All rights reserved. No part of this book may be reproduced, stored in a retrieval system, or transmitted in any form or by any means, to include electronic, mechanical, photocopying, recording, or otherwise without prior written permission of the publisher, except by a reviewer who may quote brief passages in a review.

Published by: Work Mindfulness Institute | Ingram Spark | Amazon.

Paperback (Print Edition): 978-1-7370818-2-1
Ebook (Digital Edition): 978-1-7370818-3-8
Cover Design and Interior Layout: Andy Magee
Illustration Concepts and Direction: Keith W. Fiveson

IFS™ and Internal Family Systems™ are trademarks of IFS Institute.

This work is an independent interpretation by the author and is not affiliated with, endorsed, or sponsored by IFS Institute.

All images and designs in this book were created under the artistic direction of Keith W. Fiveson using AI-assisted tools and refined in Canva.

Table of Contents

Sources & Pathways 9
   Welcome to Return of the Exiled Child:
   A Mindful Journey from Trauma to Wholeness 13

MAP OF EXILE 15
   Chapter 1: Big Mind, Breath, Witness Protector 17
   Chapter 2: Return to the Body, Memory, Rhythm, and Sacred Vessels ... 35

WALL OF ARMOR 51
   Chapter 3: Spirit: A Journey Through Breath 53
   Chapter 4: Food and Shame, Hunger, Control 71

THE INNER SANCTUARY 81
   Chapter 5: Dreams, Nightmares, and Breathing 83
   Chapter 6: Relationships, The Golden Child 93

HOUSE OF MIRRORS 111
   Chapter 7: Environment, Energy, and Coherence 113

JOURNEY HOME 133
   Chapter 8: The Arrival Home 135
   Chapter 9: The Path Forward 147

Reflection: Author's Wish 150
Afterword: Author's Note 151
Acknowledgments 152
Selected References & Suggested Readings 153

Sources & Pathways

This book reflects five universal pathways of healing: Maps of Exile, Wall of Armor, Inner Sanctuary, House of Mirrors, and Journey Home. These pathways are not spelled out in each chapter but form the underlying architecture of the work. They also appear in the Return of the Exiled Child card deck, a companion resource for those who wish to explore them more deeply.

This work is woven from the many streams of wisdom I have been fortunate to encounter over the years. Joseph Campbell's monomyth offered a map of the hero's journey, a universal pattern of exile, descent, initiation, and return that has guided seekers across time. His work revealed that the path of transformation is not linear but cyclical, a spiral through darkness and discovery toward renewal.

Carl Jung's exploration of the collective unconscious illuminated the deeper archetypal energies moving within that cycle, the child, the warrior, the sage, the lover, each a mirror of the universal psyche within every human being. Together, their teachings remind us that our personal stories are echoes of something ancient and shared, a journey as old as humanity itself.

Richard Schwartz's Internal Family Systems (IFS) model gave language to that inner world of parts, protectors, exiles, and guides, the living archetypes of our own internal myth. Taoist teachings, the writings of Lao Tzu, Zen practice, and the art of breathing revealed the way of balance and flow, teaching that healing is not the conquest of the self but its harmonization. Jon Kabat-Zinn's mindfulness-based stress reduction taught me how presence itself can be medicine. Narrative therapy traditions reminded me that while we live inside stories, those stories can also be retold, reframed, and somatically healed.

Stanislav Grof's transpersonal psychology and explorations of expanded states of consciousness opened a wider horizon of what it means to be human, reminding me that breath, body, and psyche are inseparable from the larger field of life.

These teachings have shaped my path, but the responsibility for how they are woven here is mine alone. I am not a licensed Internal Family Systems therapist, nor do I formally represent any of these authors or traditions. What you will find in these pages is my own lived integration, a mindful synthesis of the mythic, the psychological, and the spiritual, drawn from experience, contemplative practice, and dialogue with the Exiled Child within me. It is offered in the hope that it may serve as a mirror and companion on your own journey home.

Disclaimer on IFS References

This work draws inspiration from Internal Family Systems (IFS), a therapeutic model developed by Dr. Richard C. Schwartz. While IFS Institute is unable to provide individual support for independent publications, they encourage authors to ensure adherence to copyright, trademark, and intellectual property guidelines.

Accordingly, please note:

IFS™ and Internal Family Systems™ are trademarks of IFS Institute.

All references to IFS in this book are nominative and for educational and illustrative purposes only. The interpretations, practices, and integrations described herein are solely those of the author and do not represent or speak on behalf of IFS Institute or Dr. Schwartz.

Welcome to Return of the Exiled Child: A Mindful Journey from Trauma to Wholeness

Welcome to the return. Welcome home.

They are still here, waiting not for your perfection, but for your attention.

To your body
To your breath
To your spirit
To your mind
To the child you left behind

You are not reading a story
You are returning to your own home.

Let that land.

This book is a reflective journey through what I've lived, witnessed, and practiced. It is part memoir, part map, guided by the rhythms of story, teaching, reflection, and practice. Within these pages, you'll encounter internal parts, archetypes, and invitations to soften your own armor and listen more deeply. Some stories arise from my personal path, others from clients and fellow travelers. All are offered in service of your own return to wholeness.

This is not a linear path, because healing rarely is. It spirals, returns, and repeats itself until we're finally ready to listen. You may find yourself walking through the same insight more than once, but each time with new eyes.

Sometimes, we meet someone who holds us with the presence we never received. Other times, we are called to offer that presence to another, and in doing so, we begin to heal ourselves. Whether through rupture or repair, relationships challenge us to become more whole.

> *Carl Jung once wrote – "What remains unconscious will be lived out in our relationships as fate."*

Internal Family Systems (IFS) deepens this truth, showing that these internal dramas, our managers, protectors, firefighters, and exiles, don't just live inside.

They show up across the dinner table, in boardrooms, in the silence between lovers. In the crucible of connection, our parts come alive.

And it is there, in the reflection of another, that we may finally glimpse the child we abandoned.

Looking back, as I began reconnecting with my own Exiled Child, I discovered that many of the wounds I thought were mine alone were actually relational. They shaped how I formed attachments, sought safety, withheld trust. I learned that relationships are not just the settings of our pain, they are often the mirrors that reveal it.

> But healing is not a solo act.
> Presence heals.
> Resilience empowers.
> Mindfulness transforms.

Each chapter will guide you into a sacred terrain of the Self. You'll explore how the body, mind, and spirit carry not just wounds, but wisdom. You'll be invited to breathe more fully, feel more deeply, and live more authentically. You'll be asked to listen, to question, and to imagine a life with less armor and more presence.

This is an invitation. Not to read, but to remember. To reclaim what you may have left behind. To turn inward and reparent the parts of you that once felt exiled.

> You are not alone if you've ever felt lost, broken, or unseen.
> You are not beyond healing.
> It is not too late to return, and embrace your Exiled Child.

This spiral, rooted in the Latin *spirare*, to breathe, is a sacred rhythm: inhale and exhale, contraction and expansion, inward turning and outward expression. Like the breath, this work begins at the center and moves outward, expanding in waves of awareness and compassion.

So, at the end of each chapter, and at any moment of pause, return to the breath. Return to yourself and welcome yourself home.

Let this symbol be your cue.
Breathe in. Breathe out.
Return to center.

Map of Exile

"Every exile begins with forgetting the moment we lose the sound of our own voice. To return, we must first trace the map of where we vanished."

– Keith W. Fiveson

Chapter 1:
Big Mind, Breath, Witness Protector

👣 Story: The Closet, the Breath, and Mr. Moto

Before we begin each story, it is essential to understand a key idea: This book uses archetypes, named inner figures, and characters to explore parts of the Self. These are not for clinical diagnoses or IFS labeling. They are symbolic expressions, a psychodrama of how the; psyche responds to life's challenges. You'll meet figures like Mr. Moto, Jason, Tom, Sarah, the Golden Child and Willy, the main characters of this story's narrative. Think of them as roles in an inner drama, shaped by pain, protection, or purpose.

Let us begin. . . .

The dark closet smelled of mothballs and old leather shoes. He pressed his back against the wall and pulled his knees to his chest, trying to disappear. Outside, voices clashed, sharp and frantic, rising and falling, crashing waves of screams, yelling, loud and angry. His father's rage filled the air, his mother's silence, then screaming. He wanted to escape, but he was three years old, where could he go?

The tiny closet felt like a sanctuary, a place of refuge. His clothes clung to his skin, and his breath was shallow and quick. In the silence, he could hear his heart pounding like a drumbeat. His body was ready for action, to run, fight, hide, but there was nowhere to go.

He closed his eyes and listened to his breath, his chest's rhythmic rise and fall. In this quiet space, he created peace within him. Slowly, he shifted focus to the inhale, drawing in a fragile sense of calm. "It's okay, shhh . . . " "It's okay," he whispered, mimicking the soothing tone of a mother comforting her child. With every exhale, he released a fraction of the fear that had ensnared him, as if he could breathe it away.

That was the day he realized his split, his dissociative personality tendencies, Willy stayed hidden in the dark, and someone else stepped forward to think fast, stay alert, and keep him safe. He didn't know his name then, but he came to call him Mr. Moto, his imaginary witness, guide, Breath-Walker. In that moment, his mind became a refuge; thoughts became his shield. What began as a child's survival instinct would, decades later, become his most incredible tool for resilience and healing.

Later, during a quiet moment of contemplative reflection, something shifted. With eyes closed and breath steady, he returned, not to bliss, not to resolution, but to the closet. He saw the boy again, knees drawn to his chest, eyes wide and distant. And this time, the man didn't run or rationalize. He sat beside him. He didn't try to fix it. He didn't try to change the past. He simply placed his hand gently on the child's shoulder and whispered, "It's okay. I'm here now." And in that moment, the child exhaled. Not because the fear was gone, but because he wasn't alone with it anymore.

🪶 Teaching: Exploring Inner Archetypes: Unlocking the Journey to Self-Integration

This presence Willy came to know is what Zen practice calls Big Mind, not as a distant or impersonal awareness, but as an intimate and compassionate re-parenting of the Self. It is the energetic presence of Big Mind, the ever-present witness, the stillness that holds space for the wounded child within us, the one who reappears in moments of pause. The Buddhist practice of mindfulness is not just a practice to meditate; it is a survival mechanism to evolve. Calming, compassionate, connected self-breathing becomes an anchor, a lifeline to balance in an unbalanced world. Every mindful breath creates space around pain, space to soothe, to calm, and care for what is really going on inside.

In the Internal Family Systems (IFS) model, this spacious, calm, and connected presence is called **Self**, the compassionate core that can relate to all parts without judgment. As we move toward integration, it's this Self-energy, what Willy called "Mr. Moto" or Big Mind that guides and provides spacious awareness to follow the path forward.

Our evolution is based on stimulus, reaction, and the formation of events or circumstances that create our moment-to-moment existence. Within each of us are patterns, personas, and voices that emerge in response to life. These aren't random, they're archetypes, inner characters shaped by our history, wounds, and aspirations as they arise. In the space between stimulus and response we can make a choice to battle or move beyond fear, ignorance, anger, or aversion.

We all know these characters, even if we haven't named them. The inner critic. The pleaser. The strategist. The rebel. The healer. The warrior. They're not flaws, they're forms of intelligence, forged in survival, and refined through repetition. What Willy felt all those years had names: Exiles, Managers, Firefighters, Protectors. They were all a part of Internal Family Systems (IFS), where we can see these parts as protective or exiled aspects of ourselves, designed to protect our core. Managers try to control chaos, Firefighters rush in to soothe pain, and Exiles hold the burdens of early wounds..

These parts can dominate our experience, driving reactivity and resistance when unexamined. But through mindfulness and narrative therapy, we can begin to create space to hear these voices without becoming them, to track their origins, and to tell new stories about who we are and how we heal.

This chapter introduces you to a few of these inner figures, archetypes like Willy, Sarah, Jason, Tom, and Mr. Moto, not as fictional characters but as

living energies that exist within us all in some way. They are story-carriers, each one a constellation of beliefs, behaviors, and emotional residues. They represent a few of the strategies used to belong, survive, and make a difference.

These archetypes are not fixed roles, they're fluid patterns. As we become aware of them, we create room for integration. We no longer exile parts of ourselves out of shame or fear. Instead, we listen, witness, and reintegrate, transforming survival roles into soulful expressions of wholeness. This is the heart of mindful presence. It's not just about awareness of breath or thought, it's about becoming the compassionate space where all our parts can be seen, heard, and held. This is where the real turning of the Wheel of Life begins, not on the page, but in our lives, in the quiet moments between recognition and choice, that change our conditioned responses.

Teaching-Story: The Archetypes and Parts – "The Inner Council"

Within each of us lives a council of parts, inner voices who stepped in when no one else could. Some love through control. Others through avoidance. Each carries a burden, a function, and a hope. As I worked with clients and deepened my own inner work through Internal Family Systems (IFS) and archetypal exploration, these parts revealed themselves, not just as personal traits, but as universal patterns. They echoed what Joseph Campbell called the monomyth, the Hero's (or Heroine's) Journey. Each held a unique role and voice, often working tirelessly to keep the Exiled Child hidden and safe. Throughout the stories that you read you will meet the following "Inner Council" of parts.

- **Willy – The Exiled Child**
  Sensitive and shadowed, he carries the weight of unmet needs, shame, and wonder. He disappeared early, but his presence never fully left.

- **Sarah – The Over-Responsible Caregiver**
  She anticipates everyone's needs while ignoring her own. Driven to keep peace, she says yes when she means no, believing her worth depends on holding it all together.

- **Tom – The Rational Strategist**
  He relies on logic, plans, and perfection to avoid chaos. Calm on the surface, he's often holding his breath, managing vulnerability through control.

- **Jason – The Numb Armor**
  He avoids pain by numbing out, through work, distractions, or escape. Beneath the detachment is a longing to feel alive again. He makes things happen and puts out fires.
- **Mr. Moto – The Breath-Walker**
  A quiet, observant guide who leads through presence, not performance. He doesn't protect; he reminds. He brings the breath back when the noise is too loud.
- **The Golden Child – The Remembered Self**
  He waits, not as a rescuer, but as a presence. He flickers in moments of stillness, of hope, of unguarded laughter. He is the dreamer, the healer, the part that knows who we truly are.

Mindfulness didn't exile these parts, it reconnected them. It offered a way to pause, to listen, to question old beliefs and survival strategies born in another time. Many of these patterns were useful once, but now quietly limit our growth.

Are we bracing for disaster like Tom, always planning for the worst? Are we stuck in shame like Jason, haunted by past failures, or misses? Mindfulness helps us ask: *Is this true? Who is speaking? Do I still need this strategy?*

This is the turning point. Not because the parts vanish, but because we finally see them. We distinguish past from present. We move from reaction to response. And in that space of awareness, mindfulness, we begin to unwind the deeper forces, what Buddhists call the three poisons: ignorance, craving, and aversion, the core drivers at the heart of the Bhavachakra, the Wheel of Life, detailed at the end of this chapter.

This is the beginning of return.

👣 Story: The Body Remembers What the Mind Forgot

Willy was born an only child, not just in fact, but in feeling. A boy formed from secrets, caught between a man who lived a double life and a woman who had learned to carry shame like a second skin. Even as a toddler, Willy could hear and feel the longing and pain they couldn't name. So, he escaped to the stillness and silence of the closet, to his breath, from the parents who just needed to escape each other.

Two years later, when Willy was five years old, his Mom and Dad escaped through divorce, and Willy's world was literally on fire. The Brooklyn apartment that he lived in with mom was in flames. She fell asleep, drunk, a cigarette in her hand, and like a bad dream the sirens blared and he was out of bed following strange voices, crawling barefoot from his bedroom. He saw the flames climbing up the walls of the apartment ceiling. The scene was erratic, a mess of heat, smoke, coughing, and confusion. His heart pounded. His breath stopped, and at that moment, his body froze again, just like in the closet, and his mind escaped somewhere far away from his body. He split his awareness from sensation to fight, flight, freeze, and fawn, a trauma response and path that Willy's nervous system would return to in moments of fear, pain, or emotional overwhelm. Mr. Moto was there again, helping him, guiding him to hold his breath, to be the watcher rather than a feeler.

The fire didn't just consume the apartment, it burned the fragile sense of security Willy had managed to stitch together. In the days that followed, his mother was hospitalized, and he was sent away from their Brooklyn apartment to live temporarily with his estranged grandmother, aunt, uncles, cousins, people he barely knew. One of them called him a little "jew-boy" and while he didn't know what that meant, it felt strange, and he felt bad. His comfort and routine, already fragile, were gone, along with his toys, bed, and even the faint familiarity of his mother's presence, all lost. He lived in that disorientation for a few months, clinging inwardly to his Mr. Moto, and breathing, to find a sense of belonging. It was yet another fracture in the container held his developing sense of Self. Once again, he was left to rely on inner protectors to feel any semblance of control or safety. Attachment had ruptured again, and his nervous system encoded the lesson: **you're on your own.**

Teaching: Big Mind: A Spacious Way of Seeing

To look back, to see and understand, it is helpful to practice Big Mind, or spacious awareness without judgment. It's what remains when we stop identifying with every thought, every fear, every story. We zoom out and unburden ourselves. It's not passive or detached, it's deeply present. Spacious. It sees the whole picture: the scared child, the shouting parent, the trembling body, and it holds all of it without collapsing.

Zen teachers sometimes describe the Big Mind as magnanimous, or even as a parental mind, the kind of presence that doesn't pick sides, doesn't rush to fix, it just sees and stays. It's not some mystical escape hatch. It's the part of us that says, "Yes, this too belongs," even when it hurts. Big Mind is what shows up when we let go of needing to be right, or safe, or certain, and choose instead to be real. It's the breath that steadies us when we want to run. It's the pause between reaction and response. It's the wide, clear sky that holds all weather. And the beautiful thing is, it's always there.

Just like so many who deal with trauma. The closet was real, and so was the fear. Willy shivered in that tiny, dark space.

Willy didn't know at the time that he was forming the beginning of a lifelong relationship with breathwork and **mindfulness**, yes, but also with a system of inner protectors, managers, and archetypes designed to guard him from ever feeling powerless again.

We can recognize these protective patterns that we all share, by integrating frameworks like Internal Family Systems (IFS), archetypal theory, and narrative myths. Think of Joseph Campbell's Hero's Journey or Carl Jung's notion of the shadow and the personas we wear. Each system described the same truth: When trauma strikes, a part of us retreats, and others step forward to guard the wound. Protect, serve, heal, and hide from those who don't serve or lift you, to cover the cold with armor.

👣 Story: The Art of Escape

Willy learned to survive by armoring up, running, and disappearing. By sixteen, he was slipping out the back door on Friday nights, backpack slung over one shoulder, chasing the pulse of summer, the beat of the '70s, and something that felt real. The bus and train to New York City became his escape route, the clacking rails a kind of mantra, carrying him away from the suffocating silence of suburbia, his father's temper, and the black-robe judgment that never seemed far behind.

He wasn't looking for trouble. He was looking for attention. For recognition. For proof that he still existed. One night he found both at The Bitter End Café, where Curtis Mayfield played in the background and *Superfly* was on everyone's lips. These weren't just runaway episodes. They were rituals of remembrance, ways of saying, *I'm still here.*

In the 1970s, slipping into the city like a shadow wasn't just an act of rebellion. It was initiation. Platform shoes. A backpack. Ziggy Stardust eyes. He told stories, wore personas. Pretended to belong. And in that pretending, he felt seen, even if only for a fleeting moment. At home, he was the broken boy with secrets. In the city, he became someone else.

But trauma doesn't disappear when ignored. Like a dormant virus, it waits, emerging later in collapse, sabotage, or emotional spinouts. Not to punish. To protect. Willy wasn't just lying to others. He was concealing a pain too raw to name. The nervous system had encoded exile, so even in moments of stillness, chaos was never far behind.

Teaching: The Exiled Child Narrative

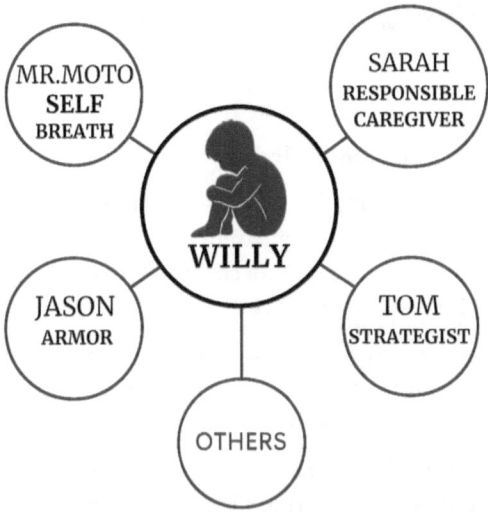

In psychology, a "constellation of parts" in Internal Family Systems (IFS) therapy represents the sub-personalities in a person's psyche, each with distinct feelings, beliefs, and functions.

As shown in the diagram, Willy does not live in isolation but within a constellation of parts, each arising to carry what the child could not hold alone, formed in reaction to the exile itself. They each have a role to play. Some distract. Some defend. Some pretend. Each one arises to help carry what the child cannot hold. And each carries a piece of the truth.

Willy, like many of us, found early refuge in the mind. When the world became too loud, too dangerous, too confusing, his thoughts became hiding places. The mental escapes were adaptive, even brilliant, but they weren't free. They came with loneliness. With the loss of play. With the burial of his own needs.

The first presence to emerge was Mr. Moto, the Breath-Walker, not a protector, but a witness, a guide. He brought breath and stillness. The subtle permission to feel. In time, other parts stepped forward.

Sarah, the over-responsible one, didn't show up in the heat of chaos, she arrived in the aftermath. She cleaned up what others couldn't name. She kept

everything working. She said yes when she meant no. She kept him useful, careful, invisible. She made survival look like success.

More parts followed. Jason. Tom. Others still unnamed. Each part became a mask, a role, a response. Together, they formed the architecture of survival. They weren't wrong. They were necessary.

But survival is not the same as living.

Through mindfulness, Willy began to witness them, not as flaws or pathologies, but as loyal companions. Some were tired. Some were afraid. All of them were waiting for someone to see them clearly. To thank them. To witness them and invite them into a new way of being.

This witnessing wasn't just therapeutic, it was sacred. It echoed a deeper map of reality he would later recognize in the **Wheel of Life**, the Bhavachakra. A symbol not only of suffering, but of choice.

At the center of that wheel are the forces that keep us spinning ignorance, craving, and aversion. Around them swirl the roles we play, protectors, performers, addicts, achievers. And beneath it all is a quiet possibility: that we are not just parts. We are not just reactions. We are not just the exile. We are also the breath. The presence. The choice to come home.

PRACTICE & REFLECTION:
Find Your Exiled Child

The Exiled Child is the part of us that holds the original wound, the first truths we were told we could not speak, the first needs we were told were too much.

They are the soft voice silenced by survival. They carry our longing, our wonder, our shame.

In the language of Internal Family Systems, they are the Exiles, tender, burdened, and hidden away to protect the system. But in the deeper mythos of our lives, they are also the sacred witnesses, the ones who remember who we were before the world demanded we become someone else.

The Exiles are not weak. They are truth-bearers. They are not broken. They are waiting. As we close this chapter, take a few moments to reflect on the inner voices that shaped your survival, and may still shape your present. Meet them. Question them. Welcome them home.

MAP OF EXILE

1. Willy - The Exiled Innocent
- When have you heard your own "Willy" whisper? What does your inner child need to feel safe today?
- What part of you has been hidden or silenced, waiting for permission to return?

2. Mr. Moto - The Breath-Walker, Guide, The One
- When have you heard your inner guide calling you to go in a specific direction?
- Who do you turn to for guidance and support when you're scared, lonely, or afraid?

2. Tom - The Rational Strategist
- Where do you over-manage or overthink as a strategy to feel in control?
- Can you identify a moment when logic became armor instead of a tool?

3. Sarah - The Resigned Caregiver
- Are you constantly tending to others while neglecting yourself?
- What would it mean to offer yourself the same care you offer others?

4. The Golden Child - The Integrated Self
- What would it mean to believe you are enough, without having to prove or perform?

5. The Exiled Child (You)
- What memories or moments have you pushed away to survive?

♋ Teaching-Practice: The Wheel of Life

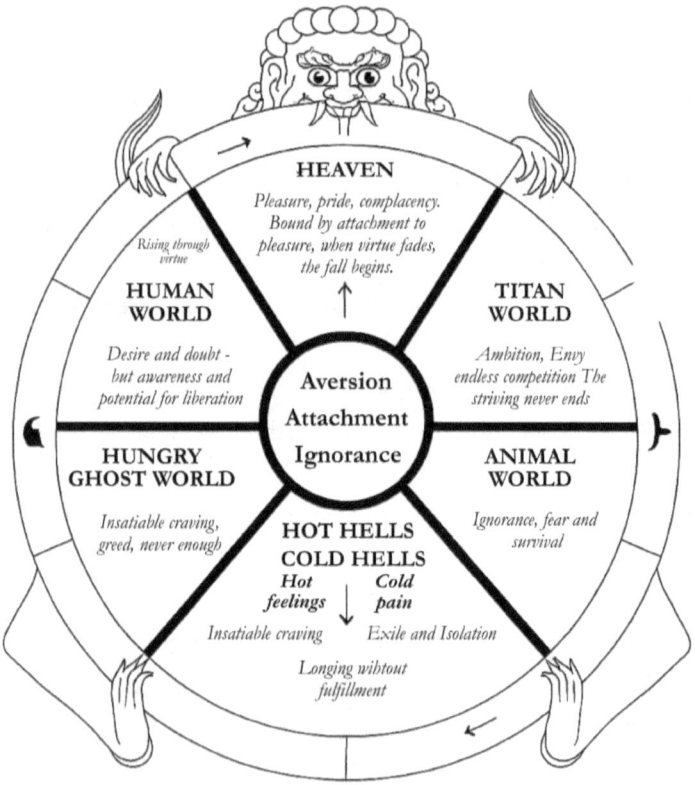

Bhavachakra - The Wheel of Cyclic Existence

A Buddhist map of cyclical existence (samsara) held within the grasp of impermanence. The six realms represent states of being-psychological, spiritual and emotional-through which the self journeys until awakening frees it.

This image is one of the visual representations of the Bhavachakra, the ancient Buddhist Wheel of Life. At its core are the three poisons, ignorance, attachment, and aversion, forces that propel the wheel upward or downward. Each moment, each choice we make, sets the wheel in motion, yet we are not bound by its momentum. The upper realms represent connection, light, and blessings, the gifts of words, food, shelter, clothing, and love, both for us and others. Here, beings exist in the Human, Heavenly, and Titan Worlds, realms of abundance and extravagance. Below, in the lower realms, dwell the Animal,

Hell, and Hungry Ghost worlds, where suffering and longing take hold in fear, doubt, and disparity. The character that holds the wheel is Yama, who represents impermanence, emphasizing that everything within the wheel is subject to change through a cycle of death and rebirth. Despite his fearsome appearance, Yama is not considered evil in Buddhism, but rather a protector of the Dharma. Dharma is the natural way of things, your soul's purpose, your inner compass. It's not just what you do, but how you live with integrity, awareness, and service to something greater than yourself.

Mindfulness is the hub, the core of the wheel. It is presencing of the now, aware of stimulus, pausing before response. To pause, breathe, and choose, determines the direction the wheel is turned. The wheel may shift upward, toward life, compassion, wisdom, and liberation, or spirals downward, toward death, deepening cycles of pain, bewilderment, and confusion.

The figures, archetypes, realms, and characters within this wheel are not separate from us, they are "us": the Exiled Child, the overwhelmed parent, the inner critic, and the watchful guide. Each facet of our psyche plays a role in the wheel's movement. By bringing them into conscious awareness, we create space for healing and transformation.

Practice & Reflection:
The Gap Between Stimulus and Response

"Between stimulus and response, there is a space. In that space is our power to choose our response. In our response lies our growth and our freedom." - *Viktor E. Frankl*

Exercise: Turning the Wheel with Awareness

Pause: Consider a recent moment when you *reacted* instead of responded. Perhaps you raised your voice, shut down, or spiraled into self-doubt. Notice the emotional charge of that moment.

Breathe: Inhale slowly for a count of 4. Hold for 2, Exhale for 6. Repeat 3 times. Let the breath anchor you in the present.

Recognize:
- What emotion was driving your reaction?
- Which inner archetype or part of you was in charge?
- (Was it the Worrier? The Critic? The Protector?)
- What belief was underneath your reaction? Was it true?

Respond: Ask yourself:
- What would a mindful response look like in that moment?
- How might I speak or act if I were guided by presence rather than fear or habit?

Rehearse: Imagine yourself responding differently next time. Visualize the choice. Feel the shift in your body. Allow that new pattern to imprint itself gently.

In the next chapter, we journey into the sacred landscape of the body, where memories are stored in muscle, scars, breath, and heartbeat, and where healing begins not in words but in awareness.

Practice: & Reflection
Mapping the Architecture of Survival

Here the concept of a "Council of Parts" in IFS mirrors Jung's idea of the psyche as a collection of autonomous complexes. Creating safety for the Exiled Child's return and the Golden Child's exaltation involves fostering a compassionate and understanding inner dialogue among these parts or archetypes.

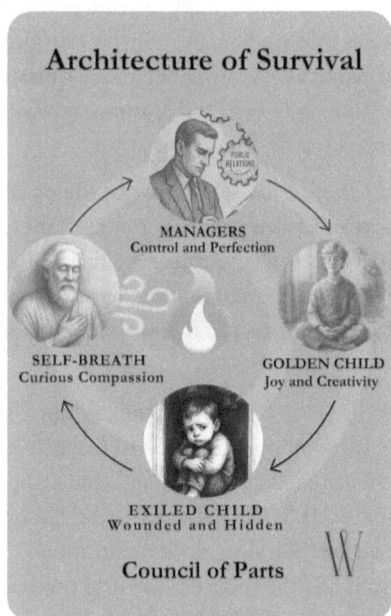

Within the Internal Family Systems (IFS) framework, protectors are understood as parts that have taken on specific roles to shield the Core Self and other vulnerable parts, like the Exiled Child, from pain and overwhelm. These protectors, such as the Manager (focused on control and perfection) and the Firefighter (reactive and impulsive), operate from a place of love and a desire to ensure survival. However, their extreme strategies can inadvertently perpetuate the exile of the Golden Child, the inherently joyful, curious, and creative aspect of the Self.

In a Jungian context, these protector parts can be seen as complexes or subpersonalities that have developed to manage perceived threats to the ego. The Manager archetype might align with aspects of the persona, the social mask, striving for external validation through achievement and order. The Firefighter could manifest as the Shadow, containing repressed emotions and impulsive behaviors that erupt when triggered. The Exiled Child embodies the wounded Inner Child archetype, carrying unprocessed trauma and longing for acceptance. The Golden Child resonates with the archetype of the Divine Child, representing potential, innocence, and the inherent wholeness of the Self.

Expanding our understanding of protectors and facilitate this inner integration:

1. **Recognizing and Unblending from Protectors:** In IFS, the first step is to differentiate from protector parts, acknowledging their positive intent without judgment. This involves understanding the fears and burdens these parts carry. For example, the Manager's need for control might stem from a fear of chaos or inadequacy, while the Firefighter's numbing behaviors might be a desperate attempt to escape overwhelming emotions held by the Exiled Child. In Jungian terms, this is about becoming conscious of the complexes and understanding their origins in personal history and archetypal patterns. Healing begins by quieting the mind, by calming the default mode network, and trauma-driven narratives that surface, through breathing and self-regulation.

2. **Understanding the Exiled Child:** The Exiled Child carries the pain, fear, shame, and other difficult emotions from past experiences. These parts often feel vulnerable and believe they need protection from further harm. In Jungian psychology, this resonates with the wounded Inner Child archetype, which holds the unprocessed emotional baggage of the past.

3. **Creating Internal Safety:** For the Exiled Child to emerge and for the Golden Child to be embraced, the internal system needs to feel safe. This involves the protector parts trusting that the Self can handle the vulnerability of the exiled emotions. In IFS, the Self, characterized by the eight qualities of compassion, curiosity, calm, clarity, confidence courage, connectedness, and creativity, is the inherent healing presence within. By accessing the Self, one can offer the Exiled Child the unconditional love and acceptance it needs. Jungian work emphasizes the importance of creating a safe space within the psyche for Shadow integration, allowing the wounded aspects of the Self to be acknowledged and healed.

4. **Honoring Protectors and Renegotiating Their Roles:** Instead of trying to eliminate protectors, IFS aims to help them release their extreme roles. By understanding their fears and validating their past functions, the Self can invite them to take on new, less extreme roles that are more aligned with the well-being of the entire system, including the Exiled and Golden Child. For instance, the Manager's organizational skills can be valued without demanding constant perfection to

keep things on schedule, if nothing more. And the Firefighter's energy can be channeled into healthier coping mechanisms, like breathing, meditation, or working out at a gym. In a Jungian context, this involves integrating the shadow aspects and allowing the persona to become more flexible and authentic.

5. **Exalting the Golden Child:** As the internal system becomes safer and the Exiled Child begins to heal, the natural qualities of the Golden Child, joy, spontaneity, creativity, and trust, can emerge more freely. This is akin to reconnecting with the inherent wholeness and potential represented by the Divine Child archetype in Jungian psychology. It's about allowing oneself to experience joy and embrace life with a sense of wonder without the constant fear of being hurt or rejected.

6. **The Council of Parts/Archetypes:** Imagine an internal council where each protector part, the Exiled Child, and the emerging Golden Child have a voice and are listened to with respect by the Self. This internal dialogue allows for understanding, negotiation, and the creation of a more harmonious inner system. In Jungian terms, this reflects the process of individuation, where different aspects of the psyche become integrated around the Self, leading to greater wholeness and psychological maturity.

By understanding the dynamics of protector parts through the lens of IFS and Jungian archetypes, individuals can cultivate greater self-compassion and create the internal safety needed for the Exiled Child to heal and the Golden Child to shine. This inner integration leads to a more authentic and fulfilling life, where vulnerability is embraced, and joy is freely expressed.

Each part serves the same purpose: to shield the system from the unbearable risk of vulnerability. Jason, Tom, Sarah, the inner crew, each developed with a particular task, a distinct style of love. Some love through avoidance. Some through precision. Some through over-functioning. None are bad or villains. All are strategies. Their loyalty is profound, born in moments when no one else showed up.

But the cost of such protection is high. Joy is rationed. Spontaneity is controlled. Connection is conditional. Over time, these survival strategies become walls, not doors, traps, not tools.

Unburdening does not mean banishing these parts. It means recognizing them, honoring them, and inviting them into a new kind of relationship. A family system not led by fear, but by compassion.

> **REFLECTION:**

- What protector still believes you must be perfect to be safe?
- What would it mean to thank that part and gently ask it to step aside, just for a breath?

But breath alone was not enough.
The body would soon call him back, asking not
just to be watched, but to be inhabited.

Breathe In, Breathe Out

Chapter 2:
Return to the Body, Memory, Rhythm, and Sacred Vessels

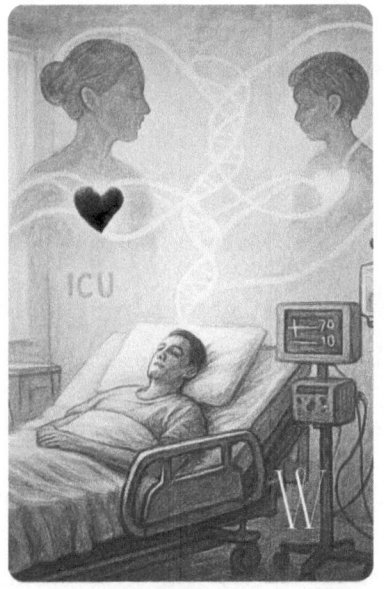

👣 Story: ICU Beeping and the Awakening of the Golden Child

Before the tubes and the wires, before the hum of machines, there was a body, his body, waiting to be heard. He was now in his late sixties, and the weight of his life pressed into the hospital bed.

Willy woke to the sound of machines.

Not just any sound, but a rhythm. At first, it was harsh, like a metallic birdsong, jagged, intrusive. But then something shifted. The beeping softened, looped. A melody began to rise beneath his haze. Led Zeppelin, *Kashmir*, he

thought, like a song he hadn't heard in years. His sternum stitched up now, opened, wired, patched like an old drum skin, humming with new tension. Tubes in his chest. Fog in his mind. His body felt like a stranger.

But the rhythm, there it was again. Not just his heartbeat, but others too. His grandmother's steady pulse as she held him as a child after his screaming nightmares. His mother's breathless humming at the sink. His father's faint voice behind closed doors. Their rhythms rose inside him like ghosts on the tide. DNA, memory, heartbeat, all one song, playing through his chest. Thoughts, memories, fantasies, as real as night and day. The ancestors of generations that gave their sweat, blood, and tears to breathe life into him.

And for the first time in decades, Willy didn't want to run from his body. He didn't hate it or wish it was smaller, tougher, or thinner. He listened. And it whispered back:

> "You made it.
> You're still here.
> *We are, too.*
> Welcome home."

꧁ Teaching-Story: Unburdening the Golden Child

Confined to the ICU for five days after surgery, Willy battled a suffocating, sterile environment. Amid antiseptic scents and the droning of machines, a profound renewal began. Perhaps it was the medication or the stillness that sparked a deeper awakening, a sense of connection to his ancestors' vibrant, resilient essence, their lineage coursing through his veins, offering solace and reminding him he was still alive.

This surgery was not an isolated event but the consequence of a much older wound. Decades earlier, the radiation that saved him from Hodgkin's lymphoma at twenty-seven had quietly scarred his heart. The valve had been weakening ever since. Now, more than forty years later, it demanded to be reckoned with.

Our bodies aren't just vehicles. They're vaults, temples, living altars. They carry scars we've earned, and some we've inherited. They tell stories we thought we'd forgotten.

Our earliest experiences of touch, how we were held, fed, scolded, or ignored, don't just shape our nervous system. They teach us whether the body is a safe place to live, whether sensation is trustworthy, whether hunger, pleasure, or softness is allowed.

For some, nourishment was fused with shame. For others, affection arrived only through performance or neediness. These early encounters with the body become the blueprint for how we inhabit it, whether we welcome ourselves home or brace against our own skin.

To be mindful of the body is to return to its sacredness, not as a machine to fix, but as a home to inhabit. It's worth remembering that within the flesh lives the spirit, and within the heartbeat, the soul, quietly pulsing with ancient knowledge.

In trauma recovery, we often speak of exiled parts, those wounded selves, banished to survive. But there is another part that hides: the Golden Child. The one untouched by shame, the Core Self. The one who waited. Not for rescue, but for permission to re-emerge.

For some, the Core Self disappears early, buried beneath neglect, abuse, and abandonment. But it never dies. It waits. Sometimes for decades. Until the body is safe enough . . . still enough . . . broken open just enough for the light to return.

As Willy lay in the ICU, surrounded by machines but held by something ancient, his lineage, he realized he wasn't alone. He wasn't just healing; he was remembering.

The body, once a battleground for survival, had become a sanctuary. And in that stillness, something deeper stirred. It wasn't just physical. It was existential, like giving birth to a newborn: pure, angelic, free of sin, fully accepting.

What returned wasn't just his Core Authentic Self, it was a part of him, a beaming golden light, that had always been there, quietly waiting, like a deeper rhythm, or a pulse beneath the pulse.

As he listened more closely, he began to sense the architecture of something greater: a layered self, composed not only of tissue and trauma, but of soul and spirit. One was still, the other moving; one held memory, the other carried breath. In the pages ahead, I will pause to explore the subtle but vital distinction between soul and spirit, and why it matters for the journey home.

Teaching: Soul, the Alter of Spirit

In mindfulness practice and contemplative reflection, it's helpful to distinguish between soul and spirit as two complementary aspects of human experience. The **soul** can be understood as the foundational essence, the seat, of who we are, a quiet, enduring presence that connects us to our ancestry, our values, and a deeper sense of being.

It is the soul that holds memory and meaning, anchoring us in a timeless awareness of the steps that preceded, existing beneath thoughts, identities, and experiences. In contrast, the **spirit** represents the dynamic, animating force that propels us forward, to step further. It is expressed through breath, voice, movement, and creativity. While the soul provides stability and rootedness, the spirit brings vitality, direction, and expression. When we sit with grief, that's soul; when we take a new breath to move forward, that's spirit..

Both elements are essential. The soul offers a kind of internal compass, reminding us of our belonging and purpose. The spirit gives us the energy and will to engage with life, pursue growth, and create meaning. In the context of healing, trauma recovery, and mindful living, recognizing this dual structure allows us to address both our need to be grounded and our drive for transformation. Practices that involve breathwork, sensory awareness, and embodiment can support the integration of soul and spirit, helping us move from fragmentation toward wholeness. Mindfulness, in this light, becomes not just a stress-reduction technique but a holistic practice that helps us reconnect with both our deepest roots and our natural capacity to heal, grow, and evolve.

> **The Soul Remembers what Spirit forgets.**
>
> The return of the Exiled Child isn't marked by fanfare or grand epiphany. It's quieter than that. It arrives like breath, subtle, sustaining, steady.
>
> As the defenses loosen and survival relaxes its grip, something else is allowed to surface. What comes forward is **not a "new self," but a remembered one.** In the Internal Family Systems (IFS) model, this re-emergence is often recognized through the presence of the 8 Cs of the True Self, qualities that live beneath the fragmentation, always available, never destroyed: These are not moral trophies to be earned. They are indicators of restoration.
>
> **Calm. Curiosity. Compassion. Confidence. Clarity. Courage. Creativity. Connectedness.**
>
> Each one a facet of your essence, untouched by trauma. Each one a signal that the Golden Child is not gone, only hidden. When the soul remembers, and the Exiled Child begins to feel safe again, these qualities start to show themselves. Not all at once. Not perfectly. But enough to feel like you're coming home to a golden light that guides and leads with breath, space, warmth, and grace.

Teaching: Vedic Kavach - Courage Made Visible

Willy wears a small pendant around his neck. He doesn't always touch it, but he knows it's there close to his chest, where he once learned to brace, hide, and hold his breath. This pendant is a Kavach, an ancient Vedic form of spiritual armor. It holds no spell, no promise to erase pain. It is only a symbolic reminder. A shield for the psyche.

Traditionally, a Kavach is crafted with sacred geometry and planetary blessings, designed to be worn close to the heart. It is both protection and invocation a whisper from the cosmos: You are not alone. You are part of something greater.

Willy didn't know all that when he first wore it. He just knew it felt like something to hold onto.

The design isn't merely ornamental. The four spirals curve inward toward a still point. In Vedic cosmology, they echo the balance of elemental forces. In Celtic tradition, the spiral reflects life's sacred rhythm: birth, death, rebirth, and return. At the center is stillness, the Self, not ego, but the quiet witness inside each of us. The one who watches. The one who breathes.

The Kavach speaks in the language of pattern and presence. It does not say, 'You'll never be hurt.' It says, 'You are already whole, even in your hurting.'

Willy wears it now not to keep fear away, but to walk forward with it. To feel the center within the spiral. To carry a symbol of return, even on the days he forgets how.

✿ Teaching-Story: Taoist Cosmology

In the quiet hum of the ICU, Willy began to sense this more fully, not in theory but in bone. Breath and heartbeat dance together. Memory and motion are intertwined. He remembered then what many wisdom traditions have long taught: the body is not just a container but an electrical conduit, a sacred bridge between ancestors and descendants, earth, and sky, past and present. Science now names this *epigenetics*. The study of how our lifestyle, environment, and experiences can change how our genes work, without changing the actual DNA sequence. Taoist cosmology understands life as the eternal dance of Yin and Yang, the interplay of Chi (also spelled Qi in Chinese, Ki in Japanese, and akin to Prana in Indian traditions), the vital life force that animates all beings and connects the seen and unseen worlds.

Willy felt his ancestors' heartbeats, the sense that they were alive through him. He was reminded of something more profound than memory, something cellular. This concept that science calls epigenetics conveys the idea that trauma, survival, and resilience can be encoded and passed down, like whispers written into the body's script. This wisdom has long been honored through ancestral reverence in many ancient cultures, including those that shaped Taoist cosmology. In this view, the body is not merely an individual vessel but a sacred continuation, part archive, part altar, to lay down our sense of who we are, to revere and respect.

It was in that liminal space, a portal between life and death, noise, and silence, that he remembered Mr. Moto, the Breath-Walker. His presence had walked quietly with him since childhood, a kind of spiritual guardian or inner healer whose image came into sharp focus as he lay in that sterile room. He saw him as a presence, an elder, standing with timeless patience at the edge of a hospital bed, his hand hovering gently over the chest of someone resting. There was no urgency in him, only deep attunement. He didn't need words or tools. His power came through his presence. Through stillness. Through listening.

Mr. Moto reminded him to breathe, that healing isn't always loud or dramatic. Sometimes, it is a slow return, a retuning of breath, an honoring of the

body's rhythms. He embodied the essence of Taoist wisdom: that balance is not something to be achieved but something to be felt and remembered in our being present. When given compassion and space, the body knows the score and how to find its way home.

But not all the body's memories were clear or comforting. Some lived in shadow, not in words, but in sensation. There were moments, even in stillness, when something would flicker: a tightening in the belly, a wave of heat, or a sudden shiver that didn't belong to the present. A strange ambivalence would rise, not fear exactly, not desire either, something in between. The body remembered things he had long since tried to forget.

Touch can become confusing for many of us early on. It's supposed to soothe. But when touch is coupled with secrecy, shame, or betrayal, it leaves a lasting imprint. A part of Willy learned that being wanted might mean being safe, but also that it could mean danger. That part learned to perform before it learned to trust. It smiled when scared. It charmed to survive. It used the body not as a temple, but as a strategy.

He wouldn't fully meet that part until later, when hunger took on other forms. But even now, he could feel the edges of it. The part of him that used seduction as armor. The part that blurred boundaries between longing and survival. It didn't seek intimacy, it sought escape. The sacred vessel is not a fixed destination but a living, breathing rhythm, an eternal dance between Yin and Yang, stillness and movement, contraction, and expansion. When energy flows, we are verbs: alive, expressive, and changing. When that flow is blocked, we become nouns: rigid, fixed, disconnected. Mindfulness of the body becomes more than a practice, it's an invitation to remember our ancestry, listen for the rhythm beneath our symptoms, and reconnect with ourselves to flow.

During recovery, he often found himself walking slowly through his neighborhood, letting each step reconnect him to the earth. The rhythm of his breath, the crunch of gravel, and the comforting sounds of birdsongs or distant wind chimes became small reminders that life still moved around him and within him. These gentle moments, along with breathwork, mindful movement, massage, and body awareness, began to stir something back into motion. They helped restore the flow of Qi - the vital energy or life force - bringing him back into harmony.

One of the most profound practices supporting this return to flow was the Six Healing Sounds, an ancient Taoist technique he encountered years earlier in Thailand while studying with Taoist

Master Mantak Chia. His teachings were not mystical abstractions but deeply embodied tools. He explained that each organ in the body holds a physiological function and an emotional frequency, a resonance. When the energy in those organs becomes stagnant, we carry not just physical discomfort but emotional heaviness, anger in the liver, grief in the lungs, fear in the kidneys.

Each practice helped restore Willy's relationship with the inner landscape of his body, not as a mechanical thing to be fixed but as a sacred field of memory, sensation, and possibility. In this way, healing wasn't about going back to who he was before, but about becoming more present with who he was now, with every breath, every step, every sound a step toward wholeness.

Each sound corresponds to one of the major internal organs and their associated emotional qualities:

- Sss for the Lungs, releasing grief, cultivating courage
- Shhh for the Liver, releasing anger, inviting kindness
- Who (like an owl) for the Kidneys, releasing fear, welcoming calm
- Hawww for the Heart, releasing impatience or hatred, restoring joy
- Hooo for the Spleen, releasing worry, grounding compassion
- Heee for the Triple Burner, balancing heat and coolness, harmonizing the whole body

These sounds are practiced with slow, intentional movement and coordinated breath, often paired with visualization.

Teaching: Somatic Experience.

In my healing journey and work with clients, I've seen these practices bring about subtle but powerful shifts, especially when practiced with other senses engaged. They allow us to reclaim a sense of internal dialogue, where the body and emotions are not just managed but met with reverence. For someone carrying sorrow, simply exhaling with a long "Sss" while visualizing white light around the lungs can evoke a sense of spaciousness and relief.

The Taoists understood that our organs are not just physical processors but also emotional centers. And when these centers are honored with sound, breath, and attention, we restore their function and return to a state of flow. In modern terms, you might call it somatic resonance. In older terms, it's simply remembering how to sing to yourself to heal.

From my training as a massage therapist and reflexologist, I've also learned about tsubos, or specific acupoints, along the body's meridian system that act as energetic gateways. When blocked or congested, these points can disrupt the flow of Ki (also called Chi, Qi, or Prana, the life force energy that animates all living beings), creating patterns of physical tension, emotional overwhelm, or chronic fatigue. We can gently unlock stored trauma and restore natural movement by applying intentional pressure, mindful breath, or compassionate presence to these points. Each tsubo is like a doorway, and often, healing begins with a simple knock, a breath, a touch, or a moment of still attention that says: I'm here. I'm listening.

As Bessel van der Kolk describes in *The Body Keeps the Score*, trauma is held in the body, sometimes as tension, illness, or numbness. Healing begins when we listen. We become attuned to what our bodies have been trying to say. When we resist these natural cycles, if we remain stagnant, we begin to deteriorate. But when we learn to move with them, we rediscover the art of living in harmony.

Touch is one of the most immediate and powerful modalities for healing. Unlike cognitive practices that rely on abstraction, touch engages the body directly. Whether it occurs through therapeutic massage, acupressure, or simple physical presence, intentional touch affirms our existence and can restore a sense of safety in the body. It offers a reminder that not all contact is harmful, some touch repairs, soothes, and reconnects.

If you or anyone else has had surgery, during recovery you may have experienced a hand on your shoulder, not as a clinical gesture, but as a sign of human care. That moment helped ground the body and reminded us that we are more

than the trauma felt throughout the body and psyche, that we were still alive and cared for.

Touch also provides insight into the unconscious patterns we've developed to manage stress and survive adversity. These somatic patterns, tight shoulders, shallow breath, slumped posture, are often linked to psychological archetypes formed over time. Rather than viewing these patterns as problems, it's more helpful to see them as protective strategies. They are creative responses to past environments and deserve respect and curiosity.

As we explore these archetypes in the pages ahead, we'll examine how mindful attention, compassionate touch, and body-based presence can help us engage with these patterns without judgment. Healing often begins not with analysis, but with awareness. When we meet our bodies with kindness, we begin to reintroduce movement, flexibility, and emotional resilience.

Teaching: Embodied Archetypes in Practice

Healing from trauma doesn't happen in the mind alone. It happens in the body, through movement, through stillness, through breath. The body remembers what the mind forgets. And the patterns we develop to survive? They live in our muscles, our posture, our reactions.

I've worked with many clients whose survival strategies became ingrained as parts, archetypal patterns born from fear and pain. These aren't broken parts. They're intelligent, adaptive responses to a world that once felt unsafe. Dissociation, performance, vigilance, each is a form of love, protection, and strength.

But these protective forms can become prisons when we no longer need them.

What begins as a part, a manager, a protector, a wounded child, can evolve into something larger. Something universal. The King. The Queen. The Magician. The Lover. The Warrior. These aren't distant ideals. They are postures of the soul, waiting to be re-inhabited with compassion and courage.

Eva – The Dissociative Wounded Healer

Eva was a former dancer, lithe and graceful, but living with chronic pain. When she spoke of her past, her eyes would drift, and her body would stiffen, gone before the words even finished. In therapy, she learned to come back through the breath. To reclaim her body, one inhale at a time. Her body became her ground, not her escape.

Maria – The Performing Wounded Healer

Maria was radiant in the hospital, a night nurse full of jokes and warm smiles. But her brightness concealed a fear of being truly seen. Behind the performance was a tender part of her that longed to be accepted without applause. Her healing came when she dared to be quiet, to stop performing, and let others hold space for her.

Barbara – The Hyper-Vigilant Protector

Barbara was the one who always knew what others needed, before they asked. She was alert, kind, and never caught off guard. But her body was tired. Years of scanning for danger had taken their toll. Her shoulders never dropped.

Her healing began when she realized she could still care without always being on guard.

These aren't just stories. They are reflections of the archetypes in all of us, parts that long to evolve. When we honor their purpose and invite them to transform, we begin to reclaim our power. We don't discard these parts. We reassign them. We ask, gently: *What role do you want to play now?*

Teaching: From Patterns to Archetypes

Eva, Maria, and Barbara's stories reveal something deeper than individual behavior; they point to shared patterns rooted in human survival. Dissociation, emotional performance, and hyper-vigilance aren't personal flaws. They are protective strategies born from uncertainty and shaped by pain. But over time, these strategies can harden into identities that block our growth. Recognizing this opens the door to something more than survival, **it invites us into archetypal healing**.

THE KING OR QUEEN BRINGS STABILITY

THE WARRIOR ACTS WITH COURAGE

THE MAGICIAN INVITES CHANGE

THE LOVER EMBODIES CONNECTION

The concept of the King, Warrior, Magician, and Lover archetypes was popularized by Robert Moore and Douglas Gillette in their 1990 book, King, Warrior, Magician, Lover.

These archetypes are energetic roles, not gendered identities. From an archetypal perspective, these protective patterns mirror universal roles that exist within all of us. Beneath the over-functioning, distancing, or striving, reside deeper energies waiting to be reclaimed. These are the inner King or Queen, Warrior, Magician, and Lover, capacities not just to survive, but to lead, protect, transform, and

connect. They aren't distant ideals. They are forces within us, waiting to be awakened and integrated. When we begin to embody these roles consciously, the body shifts from battlefield to kingdom. We stop living in reaction and begin living with sovereignty. These archetypes support the return of the Exiled Child and help restore balance to the inner landscape.

- **The King or Queen** brings presence and stability. This archetype helps us create internal order, listen to the body's wisdom, and lead with dignity and clarity.
- **The Warrior** defends vitality and boundaries. This part helps us stay present, face discomfort, and act with courage.
- **The Magician** invites change. He holds paradox, sees patterns, and facilitates transformation through insight and awareness.
- **The Lover** embodies connection and compassion. This part teaches us to feel deeply, relate authentically, and soften into vulnerability.

Together, they create an inner system where the soul is no longer in exile, but sits at the center, fully present, finally home. When archetypes are integrated, the body is no longer a battlefield. It becomes a kingdom, governed by wisdom, defended by discernment, healed through transformation, and nurtured by love. In this kingdom, the soul is not in exile. It sits at the center, fully present, finally home.

And yet, even as we map these archetypes, life will call us deeper still. There are places maps cannot reach. Places that must be walked. And so, we begin the next story, not from the throne, but from the threshold of vibration.

Teaching-Story: Healing Through Sound, Music, and Vibration

In the weeks after heart surgery, when Willy was too weak to walk without help, too foggy to think clearly, and too overwhelmed to make sense of the pain, it was *music* that began to move Willy, first internally, then literally. The rhythms and melodies didn't ask him for effort. The music gave him a way back into his body that didn't require words.

One morning, still sore and stitched, he heard a familiar tune playing softly in the other room, something soulful, something old. His foot began to move, gently tapping. Then his breath lengthened. His shoulders dropped.

And before he knew it, he was standing, swaying, walking, not far, but further than the day before. That moment wasn't just physical, it was sacred. Music carried him back into motion, into hope, into presence.

Because our bodies are mostly water, we are naturally attuned to vibration. We are resonant beings, living instruments that respond not through logic but sensation. Sound travels straight to the nervous system, bypassing analysis, reaching the cells where memory lives and healing begins. From ancient chants to mothers' lullabies, sound has always been a medicine.

Some say intention and vibration can shape water at the molecular level, like Dr. Masaru Emoto's work with water crystals. Whether scientifically validated or not, the poetic truth remains: we are vessels of water listening for kindness, rhythm, and resonance. Our healing doesn't always begin with solutions, it often begins with a sound that says: *You're safe now. You can rest. You can come home. Though Dr. Masaru Emoto's findings remain controversial, the metaphor of resonance still holds symbolic truth.*

During his recovery at home, Willy found great solace in the tones of singing bowls, soft ambient tracks, and the steady rhythm of his own breath paired with simple affirmations. Music became his companion in rehab. It helped regulate his steps, held him in grief, and softened the edges of the pain. He wasn't just surviving in those moments; he was being *tuned*.

Sound doesn't need to be loud or dramatic to be healing. The low hum of a chant, the tap of a drum, and even the ambient sounds of ocean waves or wind through trees awaken something primal, something whole. Sound reminds the body of its own capacity to settle, to soften, to remember its original rhythm.

I once worked with a client who struggled with chronic anxiety and insomnia. Silence made her more anxious, but soft music helped her sleep. It reminded her of her grandmother's humming when she was a child. Through breathwork, vocal toning, and 4-7-8 breathing, she began to find her way back into her body, one breath, one tone at a time. She said she didn't cry from sadness but because she finally felt safe.

> *Words, too, carry frequency. The body hears not just what is said but how. A simple phrase, when spoken with care. You are safe. You are here. You are not alone, can shift everything. The nervous system hears sincerity before it hears syllables.*

Light, like sound, reminds the body that it's part of something larger, a rhythm, a cycle, a pulse. When words are paired with breath, sound, words, or light,

they become more than inputs, they become companions in a healing refuge. The *presence* in vibration, the *tenderness* in music, the *truth* in light, all of it works in concert to bring us home to our bodies, to ourselves.

PRACTICE & REFLECTION:
The 8 Cs of the True Self – Calm. Curiosity. Compassion. Confidence. Clarity. Courage. Creativity. Connectedness.

1. Which of the 8 C's feel most natural or familiar to you right now?
2. Which one(s) feel distant or hard to access?
3. Recall a moment in your life, recent or long ago, when one of these qualities showed up unexpectedly. What happened?
4. If you could invite just one of the C's to sit beside you today, which would it be? Why?
5. Write a brief letter *from* that quality (e.g., Calm or Curiosity) to your Exiled Child. What does it want to say?

PRACTICE: EMBODIED SOMATIC HEALING

Body Scan with Gratitude, begin at your feet and move upward. At each point, feet, legs, belly, chest, arms, face, pause and silently thank that part of your body for carrying you. Notice sensations without judgment.

Touch and Presence Ritual, Place one hand on your heart and one on your belly. Feel your breath move beneath your palms. Stay for five minutes. Say to yourself, "This body is mine. This moment is enough."

Light Bathing, Spend five minutes in natural light. Close your eyes, breathe, and imagine the light washing through your body, clearing away tension and fatigue. Let the light remind you that healing is already underway.

Inner Smile, Loving-Kindness
Sit comfortably and gently turn your attention inward. Begin by visualizing a soft smile behind your eyes. Let that smile flow down through your face, throat, heart, belly, and limbs. Silently offer phrases of kindness to yourself, such as: *May I be safe. May I be well. May I be at ease.* Stay here for five minutes, letting warmth and gentleness spread through your body like sunlight within.

> **REFLECTION PROMPTS:**
>
> - What memories live in your body?
> - When was the last time you truly felt safe in your skin?
> - Which parts of your body have you ignored, judged, or disassociated from?
> - What sensations signal safety for you? What signals tension?
> - How might you move, breathe, or speak differently if you treated your body as sacred?
>
> These practices aren't about fixing. They are about listening, noticing, and welcoming yourself back home. As we move into the next chapter on Spirit, we will explore how breath animates us as human beings, and how to awaken the life within, one breath at a time. Breath is more than air; it is the sacred bridge between body and consciousness. It's the first thing we do when we enter this world and the last when we leave. Everything in between, every rise and fall, every inhale and exhale, is a chance to return.

WALL OF ARMOR

*"What we built to survive becomes the prison we carry.
The armor kept us safe once, but to live, we must lay it down."*
— KEITH W. FIVESON

Chapter 3:
Spirit: A Journey Through Breath

👣 Story: The Sacred Exit and Reclaiming the Breath

Willy was born between two broken worlds. His mother, baptized in the rituals of Irish Catholicism. His father, orphaned, was shaped by the silence of exile and the shadows of survival. Willy was torn, as he breathed in and out questions surrounding life and death.

Now, Willy sat at the edge of the vast ocean, wrapped in the crash of waves and the salted breeze that whispered of something ancient, like the sands of time. He was thirty-eight, years before the ICU, and the decision before him was monumental: as he bargained with a second surgery to deal with cancer. The first, at twenty-seven, had been Hodgkin's lymphoma. Back then, radiation

had saved his life, but it also left a hidden cost, the radiation damage that lay dormant. Eleven years later, the doctors had found a deadly sarcoma, seeded by that same radiation, pressing into his neck, and threatening to spread.

Surgery was the only way to achieve "clear margins," the doctors said. But the cost? His neck. His arm. His ability to move and work. More than muscle or bone, it felt like they were asking for a part of his soul. And if he refused? He'd be gone within the year.

Willy had been here before, standing on the edge of life and death, but this time, something deeper stirred. Survival alone wouldn't be enough. He didn't want just more time. He wanted a life he could fully inhabit.

Doubt clouded his mind. Could he trust the doctors? Would he ever be whole again? Beneath the medical risk was a spiritual reckoning: *Where is God in all this?*

He followed that question into action. He declined the surgery and instead sought a different path, one rooted in trust, spirit, and self-agency. He partnered with Dr. Keith Block, an integrative physician who didn't just treat his tumor, but walked beside him for five years.

Willy changed everything. He became vegan. Practiced yoga and meditation. Trained to teach. He learned to live with presence, to heal without the blade, and to rebuild not just his health, but his spirit and life.

Willy didn't know it then, but every held breath was a prayer. Every return to breath would become a step back toward Spirit.

Teaching: The Language of Spirit (SPIR):

We use the word Spirit, but what is it? The Latin root *SPIR* means "to breathe." And within that root lives a quiet power, a sequence of words that chart the journey from inspiration to integration:

Root Word	Meaning
Inspire	To breathe into life or creativity
Aspire	To breathe toward something greater
Respire	To breathe again, to recover
Perspire	To exert effort through the breath of the skin to act on Inspire and Aspire
Conspire	To breathe together
Transpire	To breathe across into happening
Expire	To breathe out one final time

Breath is not just survival. It is the story. It is a signal. It is Spirit and our ability to be with it, to watch and manage it, will allow us to be a part of every adventure.

Spirit is not bound by religion, it is breath. It is the invisible current that moves through all living things, the pulse beneath the surface of every moment. Willy came to believe that Spirit is the breath we all share, the rhythm that calls us inward, toward memory, meaning, and sometimes, toward the parts of ourselves we've left behind.

It is the quiet rhythm of breath that calls the Exiled Child home.

👣 Story: Willy's Inherited Exile

Willy was born into contradiction. His Irish Catholic mother baptized him in saints and sacraments, a lineage of displacement and resilience. His Latvian Jewish father, hardened by childhood abandonment and silence, carried the grit of a survivor, an orphan, a fighter, a man shaped by secrets and the streets. Willy was the bridge between them, raised between two wounded worlds and belonging fully to neither. He learned to survive in silence. To hold his breath. To shrink his body so it wouldn't make noise.

The silence only thickened when his mother remarried. Her new husband, John, was unpredictable and violent. A sideways glance, a bottle of vodka, or a muttered question, like *What do you want?* could erupt into chaos. Willy's nights blurred into each other: police sirens, slammed doors, screams that no one could unhear.

Then came the night that changed everything.

The kitchen lights were bright. His mother stood frozen in fear. Willy's small hand trembled around the handle of a steak knife he didn't remember picking up. But he had. The strike. The run. Out the door. Into the night.

Back into the closet – *Shhh . . . it's going to be okay.*

That night was the last time he saw his mother and John. Soon after, he was sent to live with his father in the suburbs. Exiled again. Another rupture.

It would take decades before Willy understood what had truly vanished that night. Not just safety, or connection, or even childhood, but the sacred thread of breath itself. His sense of Spirit. Not religion. Not dogma. But presence. Innocence. Life's rhythm pulsing at the center of the soul. Spirit hadn't abandoned him. But to survive, Willy had abandoned spirit. Willy's breath disappeared to survive. In its absence, something sacred was lost, not just safety, but connection to Spirit, the rhythm of being. That loss shaped what came next. . . .

Story: Tom – The Rational-Military Strategist
Willy disappeared to survive. Tom polished himself to perform.

One held his breath to stay unseen; the other measured it to stay in control. Where Willy vanished into silence and fear, Tom rose with structure and strategy. Both had lost their connection to Spirit, one through raw panic, the other through ritualized precision.

But even then, something remained. A whisper. A witness. **Mr. Moto**. He wasn't a rescuer, but a breath between them, the quiet presence that neither froze nor performed, but simply noticed. That still point in the storm, waiting to be remembered.

If Willy was the boy crouched in the closet, Tom was the man behind the desk, suit pressed, laptop open, decoding pain into performance. He didn't run. He strategized. He structured. He succeeded.

But his breath? It was always controlled. Always measured. The kind of breath you take when you don't trust the room. Or yourself. Willy disappeared to survive. Tom perfected himself to stay safe. Both exiled parts. Both cut off from spirit, not as theology, but as the animating rhythm of life itself.

While he served in the Army, Willy relied on Tom, the rational strategist, who didn't feel. The stoic, he decoded. And in the hum of machines and the click of encryption, his breath became the only thing still human.

The hum of the server room was oddly soothing. Deep inside a secured communications bunker, Tom sat under dim blue lights, eyes flicking between glowing screens and printouts of encrypted messages. Outside, it was desert-dark, command headquarters. Inside, it was all business, precision, silence, structure.

He had a job to do: decode, assess, deliver. One wrong interpretation could lead to lives being lost. There was no room for emotion, only protocol.

Amid switchboards and communications gear, he adjusted his headset and keyed in a sequence, breathing in through his nose and out through his mouth. Even then, before he had words for it, breath was how he stayed composed. It was his hidden practice, the one thing that kept his mind from slipping into memory.

Because outside the codes, there was another kind of encryption: the image of his stepfather's leather belt on a hook . . . the sound of dishes shattering … the whispered promise to himself, made as a boy, that he'd never let chaos win again.

Tom became the strategist, the executor, the polished corporal. He was reliable and untouchable. He carried secrets for a living, national, tactical, and personal.

✦ Teaching-Story: Willy's Exile, Loss, and Burden

Willy isn't just a boy. He is the Exiled Child archetype, the one cast out not by punishment but by necessity. The part of us that holds the truth we couldn't say, the breath we couldn't take, the tears we couldn't cry. He appears in moments of vulnerability, in dreams and memories. He shows up when we sit quietly with our breath, when we return to the places where we once disappeared.

Willy doesn't want rescue. He wants recognition. To be seen, heard, and recognized for who he is. He is not broken. He is waiting. But waiting requires breath and patience. And there were chapters in Willy's life where breath left him again, this time, not in childhood, but in the ruins of adulthood.

Like when his mother died from alcohol poisoning at fifty-one. A woman made of both steel and softness, she had endured more than she ever admitted: three marriages, parents lost and betrayed, buried siblings, and buried pain. She died alone, grief-stricken from the loss of her innocence, her children, and her battle with alcohol. When she died, something ancient inside Willy collapsed. Her breath stopped. And so did his, for a while.

He needed to identify her body, discovered two weeks after her death in her small Brooklyn apartment, above a television store. Willy stood alone in the aftermath, leading to the collapse of his first marriage. His wife told him she was cheating, pregnant with another man's child, and getting an abortion.

Willy didn't yell or confront; instead, he turned inward, as if holding his breath for too long. His spirit crushed, he walked out the door, and filed for divorce.

He was looking back, and again remembered that it wasn't the first time the world had pulled the rug out from under him. Years earlier, at just seventeen, Willy had been kicked out of the house, thrown into the world with nothing but a bag of clothes, $20.00, and a searing ache in his chest. Days later, he was picked up for cannabis, a joint, but under the Rockefeller laws, it was a felony, enough to derail a life. He panicked, lied, said he was eighteen, and provided a fake name. The police fingerprinted him and set a date for arraignment. But there was no internet back then, no digital shadow. He vanished.

The train to New York City, where The Salvation Army took him in, no questions asked. A cot, a meal, and a job washing dishes. It was the first thread of safety he'd felt in weeks. That job eventually led him north, to a hippie commune where pasts didn't matter and futures were chosen moment by moment. There, among fields, acres, and nameless peace and love seekers, Willy began to disappear, and Jason began to come forward, living the living the life of a hippie at the Farm. Willy was still breathing, but it wasn't the breath of innocence anymore. It was the breath of armor, and another part of him was emerging, a part that had no boundaries.

Teaching: IFS Recognition to Renewal

Through Internal Family Systems (IFS), we learn that acknowledging our exiled selves, especially the child within, opens a door to compassion that invites them home. This is not just an invitation but a transformative act rooted in love and understanding. When exile is recognized, that compassion becomes a profound source of inspiration. It is the moment when the breath once held in fear becomes the breath that carries life forward, with purpose, clarity, and power.

Reuniting with Willy, recognizing the child he had left behind, did not end in stillness. It stirred something deeper, a longing not just to remember, but to awaken. This journey back to the Exiled Child was infused with compassion, spirit, and the energy of a Truer Self.

As Willy breathed more consciously into the memory of that exile, it brought grief, and possibility. Breath, once used to survive, now whispered of other potentials: to create, to express, to transform. This renewal celebrated the energy that can be harnessed when exiled parts are welcomed home, allowing the True Self to flourish again.

Teaching: Mr. Moto the Authentic Self

Mr. Moto is not a person but an archetype, the breath-born embodiment of what IFS refers to as Self-energy. He is the felt sense of calm, curious presence that arises when parts unblend and we reconnect with our core. He emerges when the system begins to regulate, the breath deepens, and protective parts step back long enough to allow presence. Each individual may encounter their version of this archetype, whether it appears as a voice, a feeling, a memory, or simply a quiet sense of knowing.

Mr. Moto symbolizes the capacity within all of us to access inspiration that is grounded in clarity, calm, and connection through breathwork and presence.

He appears not with urgency but rhythm, like the tide, like the pause between heartbeats. In this sense, inspiration is not an external force, but a **somatic and psychological readiness**. It arises when the nervous system is no longer hijacked by fear or survival-based reactions, and when the inner field becomes spacious enough to allow new ideas or impulses to emerge. Inspiration, in this model, is the movement of breath through an unburdened system.

What is Inspiration?

"To inspire," Mr. Moto would say, "is literally to breathe in." In Latin, *inspirare* means "to breathe into," not just the lungs, but the psyche, the soul. Inspiration is not about motivation in the performance-based sense. Rather, it is about **reconnection** to Self, meaning, and purpose. It is the moment when the individual no longer looks for external validation but instead opens to an internal compass.

In practice, this often happens during stillness. Many clients in somatic or IFS-informed work report moments of sudden clarity not during a

breakthrough conversation but in the silence afterward, in a deep breath, a walk by the ocean, or a meditation when nothing seemed to be happening. Mr. Moto appears in those moments, symbolizing the Self's capacity to reorganize and reintegrate fragmented parts into coherent insight or action.

From an IFS perspective, inspiration is the spontaneous alignment of the system. When parts are heard, respected, and unblended, a natural movement toward wholeness occurs. The breath itself often serves as both a metaphor and mechanism for this: deep, regulated breathing helps bring protective systems offline and reactivates the parasympathetic state, what Polyvagal Theory calls "ventral vagal" tone. In this state, the internal conditions are optimal for Self-leadership and the emergence of inspired action.

Mr. Moto's presence also reminds us that **creativity is not manufactured**; it is uncovered. It arises not from control but from coherence. He teaches that every creative act, whether it is artistic, relational, or personal, begins not in striving but in **allowing**, in creating enough inner space for the spark to ignite.

How the Self Emerges

Mr. Moto is not a typical "part" like a Protector or Exile. He represents what IFS calls **Self-energy**, or the calm, compassionate presence that can hold space for all other parts without reacting from fear or pain. Archetypally, he mirrors the **sage** or **inner guide**, an integrative force who observes, listens, and responds with clarity and breath.

Unlike parts that carry burden or defense, Mr. Moto offers a grounded presence. He does not push or perform. He breathes, witnesses, and waits. His presence signals a return to safety, a readiness to live from the inside out, in alignment with body, mind, spirit, and soul.

He is not a memory, but a rhythm. Not a solution, but a reminder: To be a human *being*, not just a human *doing*.

IFS Terms: Glossary Table for Chapter 3

This table summarizes key Internal Family Systems (IFS) terms mentioned in chapter 3, offering plain-language definitions that support the reader's understanding of the IFS model.

IFS Term	Plain Language Definition
Self-energy	Your calm, compassionate core. When you're not reacting from fear or pain, you're in Self.
Exile	A part of you that carries hurt, shame, fear, or trauma, often from childhood. These parts want care.
Protector	Protectors, which include managers and firefighters, are parts that steps in to keep you from feeling pain. Shows up as control, perfectionism, anger, or numbness.
Blending	When a part takes over and you become the emotion (e.g., shame, anxiety). Healing starts when you unblend.
Unburdening	The process where a part releases painful beliefs or memories it has carried. This opens space for healing.

Teaching: SPIRIT - Aspiration: Breathing Life into Purpose

Aspiration is the purposeful direction of our breath toward meaningful goals. It is intentional breathing, fueling dreams into tangible reality.

We all have our place at the ocean, where we contemplate life and what it means to us. We may aspire to be fit and healthy, living longer lives where we don't need a respirator or oxygen tank. But can we trust this process? Are our bodies capable of realigning themselves with breath and intention? Again, it is breathing and our sense of alignment that we are seeking, a way to connect with the flow of life itself.

People develop aspirations in many ways. Sometimes they arise from necessity, like the desire to heal or survive. Other times, they emerge from inspiration, seeing someone else achieve something great or feeling the deep pull of purpose within. Television, books, news stories, childhood dreams, personal struggles, being with others, and life-changing experiences all contribute to what we aspire to. The breath in all its simplicity, carries the

essence of aspiration. When we focus on our breath, we bring clarity to our goals. When we intentionally breathe through challenges, we strengthen our resilience and determination.

👣 Story: SPIRIT – Exhale-Decrypt, Return

Years later, Tom found himself on a rooftop in midtown Manhattan. Dusk had painted the skyline in violet and gold. His tie was loosened. His hands were in his pockets. He breathed.

It wasn't the kind of breath you take before a presentation. This was deeper. Slower. Intentional. The type of breath that finds you when you're finally ready to stop running. To drop the baggage.

The rooftop was quiet, but inside, Tom's thoughts flickered like the old screens in Army Signal Corps. Except now, there were no codes to crack. Just feelings. Memories. Questions. Who was he, really?

What would it mean to stop protecting? To take off the armor?

He placed a hand on his chest. Felt his pulse. Not the steady rhythm of duty, but something rawer, alive, uncertain, real, out of sync. Something that needed to be mapped, or decoded.

For decades, he had spoken in codes. Felt in fragments. He had encrypted his life. Now, he was learning to decrypt himself. One breath at a time. Tom inhaled deeply. He was ready to be home with Willy to do whatever was necessary.

Mindful breathing strengthens our resolve and aligns us with our deepest values and missions. By breathing with awareness, we cultivate a connection between intention and action, making our aspirations not just wishes but tangible steps toward change. Each purposeful breath we take contributes to our ability to positively impact the world around us, shaping our path with clarity and purpose.

Teaching: SPIRIT - Perspire, Manifest, Effort

Perspiration symbolizes the effort required to manifest our aspirations. Inspiration or aspirations require perspiration to manifest in the world; otherwise, they remain dreams.

Willy's life turned a corner. He embraced a plant-based way of eating, found grounding in yoga and meditation, and began to live with presence. Healing no longer required the surgeon's blade, it came from within. Piece by piece, he rebuilt not only his body but his entire way of being. The turning point was a vow: if he truly wanted to live, he had to say yes to life itself. That meant letting go of fear, refusing to be haunted by the thought of failure, and meeting each challenge as it came, no matter how steep the climb.

Surgery was a reality he could not escape, but his attitude toward it was something he could control. Change is rooted in commitment, and commitment is inherently tied to challenge. It wasn't just about hoping things would improve; it was about doing the work to ensure they did. To truly transform, he had to recognize that challenges weren't obstacles, they were opportunities to build resilience.

Through mindful effort, mental, physical, and emotional, Willy could navigate this uncertain road with strength. Every bead of sweat in the gym, every deep breath taken during meditation, and every choice to nourish his body with care were steps toward the future he wanted. His sweat symbolized his dedication, the tangible proof of his perseverance and action. Each challenge he faced made him stronger, more adaptable, and more willing to embrace change. By accepting this effort as part of his journey, he was no longer a passive observer in his own life, he was fully engaged in shaping it. Mindful effort anchored his spiritual intentions firmly in the real world, driving authentic transformation and personal evolution from the inside out.

Teaching: SPIRIT – Respire and Tone

Whatever part we play as human beings, we all breathe. Respiration embodies balance and renewal, essential to life's rhythm. To gain courage, balance, and heal, Willy incorporated every tool available to manage his autonomic nervous system, mindful breathing, sound healing and toning to stimulate his vagus nerve. The vagus nerve is a crucial component of our parasympathetic nervous system and serves as our body's internal switchboard, regulating functions such as heart rate, digestion, and emotional well-being.

Dr. Stephen Porges's Polyvagal Theory offers profound insights into how trauma, stress, and fear can disrupt our breath, triggering a fight, flight, freeze, or fawn response. According to Porges, our bodies have evolved intricate systems to respond to perceived threats. When we perceive danger, whether real or imagined, our autonomic nervous system can become dysregulated. This dysregulation manifests in our breathing patterns, leading us to experience shallow or erratic breaths that disconnect us from ourselves and each other. In these moments, we may feel trapped in a cycle of anxiety and disconnection.

However, by consciously engaging in deep, diaphragmatic breathing, thereby activating our vagus nerve, we can counter these stress responses and guide ourselves back into equilibrium. Deep breathing signals our bodies that we are safe, allowing us to relax and return to a state of balance. Porges emphasizes that social connection also plays a critical role in this process. When we are connected to others, we can regulate our nervous systems more effectively. The presence of supportive relationships helps us to navigate stress and find our way back to calm.

Through techniques such as slow nasal breathing, humming, chanting, and breath retention exercises, Willy learned to regulate his nervous system, restoring a sense of calm, clarity, and coherence. Breath became his bridge between fear and resilience, chaos and control. By mindfully managing respiration, he found a way to reclaim his body's natural equilibrium and move forward with confidence, rather than being held hostage by uncertainty.

🌀 Teaching-Story: Expire-Breath

Each breath we take is a gift, a present moment offered with no guarantee of another.

Willy remembered the sterile hush of the ICU, the rhythmic chirp of machines, the dry pull of air through the tubes that delivered him oxygen. Breath came like a whisper then, fragile, metered, precious. In that space between pain and peace, he first understood what it meant to receive a breath as if it were both a mercy and a miracle. To breathe is to say yes to life, even amid pain, even in the shadow of death. And yet, how rarely we notice it. How easily we forget that the next breath is not promised.

In illness, this awareness sharpens. The breath becomes a companion we learn to count, measure, and chase. In the stillness of hospital rooms or the hush between diagnoses, we begin to understand that each inhale is an arrival and each exhale a letting go.

To expire, to breathe out one final time, is a sacred act. In that threshold moment, Mr. Moto, the Breath-Walker, stands silent and still. He does not intervene. He bears witness, for it is not his task to stop the breath from leaving, but to honor the life it carried. He watches not with detachment, but with reverence, reminding us that even in our last exhale, we are seen. We are not alone. It is not simply the end of life; it is the final punctuation in the sentence of a soul's journey through a body. For the Exiled Child, who once learned to hold his breath to survive, the idea of expiration is not terrifying. It is clarifying. It is the promise that one day, even the burden of vigilance will be released.

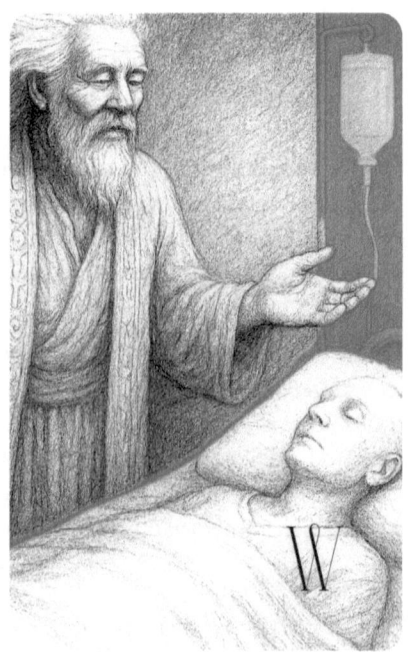

Philosophers and mystics have long meditated on the exhale as a spiritual passage. In the exhale, we surrender. In the exhale, we release control. We trust that something larger holds us. Breath teaches us this rhythm, not just in death, but in the many smaller deaths we face: the endings, the farewells, the unknowns.

Medically, expiration is a function of the parasympathetic nervous system, signaling relaxation, signaling the body's ability to downshift. But mystery lingers even in science. Why do some hold on so long? Why do others slip away in a sigh? There is something there, something that numbers and monitors can't quite explain.

Mr. Moto, the Breath-Walker, teaches us to meet each breath as if it were both our first and our last. This Self-Energy often appears during crisis, like the quiet aftermath of the ICU, after Willy's surgery. It was the kind of moment when the room is dim, and machines click steadily, when there is no voice, no flash of insight, just a presence. It could be beside the bed, and a whisper through the lungs, the sound of the breathing alone: *This, too, is sacred*. You are unburdened, there is a welcoming surrender. A witness and sacred guide, a way.

PRACTICE & REFLECTION:
Integration of Sacred

This chapter was not written to be understood by the mind alone, but to be felt, breathed, and lived. Spirit speaks not in doctrine, but in presence. And presence begins with breath.

Breath Ritual, A Sacred Practice

Set the Space:
- Light a candle or incense.
- Sit in stillness near a window or with soft ambient music.
- Place your hand gently over your chest or belly.

Breathe:
Inhale slowly for 4 counts
Hold for 7 counts
Exhale gently for 8 counts
Repeat 3–5 times

With each breath, whisper:
- *Inhale: "I return."*
- *Exhale: "I release."*

Feel the air on your skin. Notice the rhythm beneath your hand. Listen to the silence between each breath. That silence is not emptiness, it is sacred space.

Sound: Embrace Silence

Find a comfortable position, close your eyes, and take a deep breath through your nose, and exhale out your mouth. Relax and let your breath find a natural rhythm.

Now, notice the sounds around you, inside of you, and outside, in the room, the space outside, and beyond, and the silent spaces between them. Inhale, exhale, watch the space between your breathing, exhale, and release distractions.

Use this technique when you are out and about, stopping at moments where you can listen to the sounds of the space and the silence in between. Like the space between the raindrops.

> **Reflection: Return to Presence**
>
> 1. **When have you felt most connected to your breath?**
>
>   In fear? Joy? Stillness? Pain? What did it teach you?
>
> 2. **What are you still holding your breath for?**
>
>   Where are you guarded? Where do you still protect rather than soften?
>
> 3. **Can you imagine breathing as if you were already safe?**
>
>   Try it. For just a few moments. What changes in your body? In your heart?
>
> 4. **See the Exiled Child within you.**
>
>   Are they breathing? Are they hiding? How might you breathe with them, not to fix, but to be with?
>
> 5. **Offer a blessing to your breath:**
>
>   > *This breath is sacred. It connects me to every part of me I once left behind.*

Breathe In. Breathe Out.

Feel the Cool on the Inhale and the Warmth on the Exhale.

Chapter 4:
Food and Shame, Hunger, Control

👣 Story: A Table, a Nickname, the Basement

He was alone. Unseen. Unheard. Unloved. So, he turned to food to deal with his shame, secrets, and detachment from his body. Between the ages of nine and ten, they called him "fluff" because of his oversized fluffy shirts and favorite sandwiches, peanut butter and marshmallow (also known as Fluffernutters). He was overweight (fat) for much of his childhood. Always reaching for something to fill the space inside. His Dad, the king of sarcasm, would say, "I'd rather clothe you than feed you," Or worse: "You eat like you've got two assholes."

And there it was, the shame. Served up colder than any meal. Not just about the food, but also about the need for it. About having any need at all.

His mother, who struggled to be present, was the "Feeder" archetype. She would insist he eat more, "for me," she would say, believing every bite filled his stomach and heart. "You need to grow strong, Willy," she would say, "If you learn to cook and eat you'll never go hungry," urging him to indulge and enjoy food, to fill the void she sensed in him.

But it was his father's sarcasm, the "Restrictor" archetype, that seemed harsh in contrast; always slightly angry, ready to belittle Willy's appetite or nervousness with biting remarks. He was a real tough guy, convinced that discipline would "make Willy harder" and give him strength. Willy was caught between comfort and the unyielding pressure to conform. The "Feeder" and the "Restrictor." Neither could see the hunger for what it really was: the need to be whole.

The shame deepened, not merely about food but about needing love, acceptance, and space to be vulnerable. But all that kept echoing in his mind were his parents' voices, a clash of nurturing and restriction, each shaping his relationship with himself and the world around him.

But hunger doesn't always begin in the stomach. It begins in the places where needs were unmet, unseen, or shamed. Food was one way Willy tried to fill the silence, to calm the ache. But beneath that ache was something deeper, a hunger not just for sweetness, but for his safety. Not just for fullness, but for understanding, to be loved. And there was a moment, a crack in time, that shaped how he would carry his body, his shame, and his need. That moment didn't happen at a table. It happened in the basement when someone took advantage of his need.

Story: Basement-Betrayal-Shame, Hunger and Secrecy

There was a moment, a deeper moment, that locked the closet shut. A crack in time. A shift in air. Willy was eight years old; it was in the dim basement of the building he lived in, when something was taken. The boy who took it was older, thirteen perhaps. His name was Harry Black. Trusted. Familiar. He moved through the family space like he belonged.

That betrayal didn't just change how Willy felt in his body. It changed how he carried it.

It sealed the door to a deeper hunger, one unspoken, untended, and barely understood.

Willy didn't have words for what happened. No one asked. No one explained. So, in the silence, he made meaning the only way a child can: through behavior. Through protection. Through shame-wrapped patterns of detachment.

Pleasure became complicated. Touch became confusing. His body, once a place of softness and longing, became a landscape to hide, or use.

This was the birth of the Promiscuous Archetype, not born of desire, but rupture. He searched for connection through secrecy. He confused being wanted with being worthy. He learned how to disarm with his body, to be wanted without ever being seen.

He began to equate attention with safety, even when it carried shame. His hunger wasn't just for food or touch, it was for clarity. For someone to say:

"This wasn't your fault. This isn't yours to carry."

But no one said it. So, Willy carried it, into closets, cravings, encounters that blurred survival and sabotage. His promiscuity wasn't rebellion. It was reclamation. A way to say:

"I choose now." Even if part of him remained that frozen boy in a basement no one dared name.

This is where Jason began to form. Not fully formed, not yet armored, but present. The whisper of a strategy. He didn't cry. He calculated. He didn't crave. He controlled. Jason, the Numb One, the Firefighter, grew from this moment. A fast-talking mask. A charming shield. A flicker of something cool and sharp being forged in the heat of shame.

Teaching: The Hungry Ghost and the Closet

In Gabor Mate's perspective on childhood traumas, there is a critical understanding of how emotional pain often manifests physically, particularly through food-related behaviors. He discusses how children, when faced with neglect, abuse, or shame, may unconsciously turn to food as a means of comfort and self-soothing. This phenomenon suggests that food can serve as a temporary refuge, allowing children to escape their emotional distress, even for a moment. We will see how this manifest as the story progresses further.

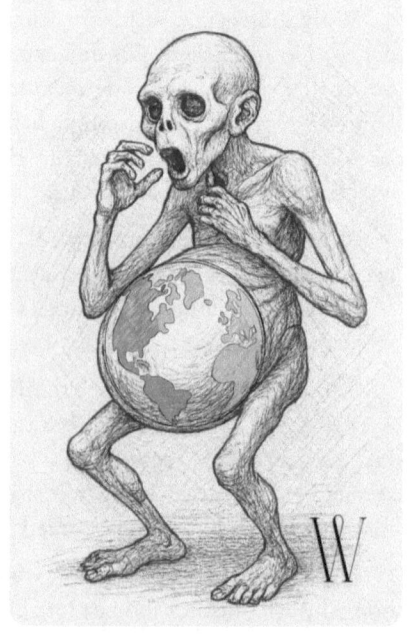

Food became a surrogate for the affection and validation he craved as a child but never received during those early years when he had to hide. It wasn't just about satisfying hunger; instead, eating took on a deeper significance. It morphed into a ritual that allowed Willy to buffer the emotional turmoil that encircled his inner world. Each bite momentarily dulls the sharp edges of sorrow and despair, creating a soothing effect that masks the fear of rejection and feelings of inadequacy.

In this way, his attention to food and eating became intertwined with his emotional state, a complex relationship that highlights not just a struggle with physical nourishment, but also signals a profound search for emotional security and connection that was lacking in his life at the time.

As we remember, Willy lived in the closet, sometimes literally. He hid, snuck snacks when no one was looking. He touched himself in the dark. He imagined wild escapes where no one could judge his body, hunger, or desire. He was the child who learned early that to be soft was to be ridiculed. That pleasure was something you had to steal. That secrets were safer than truths.

Rules didn't matter to Willy. He was the one who ran, not to rebel, but to survive.

He was the part who snuck snacks, touched himself in the dark, and dreamed of places where softness wasn't punished. He was the Exiled Child, the exiled instinct, the exiled "Willy," the raw pulse of need we are taught to bury under shame.

These parts of our psyche often develop in response to the environments we grow up in, shaping our relationships with food, others, and ourselves well into adulthood. Physician and trauma expert Dr. Gabor Maté describes this dynamic in his book *In the Realm of Hungry Ghosts*, where he explores how unresolved emotional pain often manifests as addiction, not from weakness, but from unmet needs. He highlights how struggles with food and consumption frequently stem from early experiences of emotional neglect or trauma, what he calls the "hungry ghost," an inner void yearning for connection, acceptance, and wholeness.

Our relationship with food is not just about hunger; it often mirrors our childhood wounds, coping patterns, and desperate attempts to soothe the ache of isolation. Recognizing Willy, or your own hunger, and the reasons we turn to food, becomes a turning point. It was not about discipline or willpower. It was about grief. It was about tenderness. Healing began when the need beneath the craving was named and held, not hidden in shame or mockery, but witnessed with compassion.

Our relationship with food is rarely

just about feeding the body. More often, it carries the weight of childhood memories, unspoken struggles, and the ways we've tried to survive a complicated world. For Willy, it was also shaped by the echoes of scarcity, and the constant reminders of 'children starving, a deeper awareness that half the world still goes without enough to eat. These early messages wove scarcity and injustice into his personal experience of hunger.

By acknowledging the neglected aspects of our lives, and the reasons we turn to food, or other coping strategies, we can embark on a healing journey,

making space for our emotional needs to be recognized rather than concealed beneath layers of shame or ridicule.

In Buddhist cosmology, there is also a realm called the Hungry Ghost. Bellies bloated. Mouths too small. Craving without satisfaction. The world could never be enough to fill the hole in his belly and heart. That was Willy. That is us, when we hide what we truly need. It's not just about food, it's about an insatiable craving rooted in emotional deprivation. That was Willy. That is all of us when we're cut off from what we truly need: to be seen, heard, loved, and recognized.

But here's the thing: we don't only hide food in closets. We hide desire, shame, sexuality, and longing. We hide our true selves. Hiding these insatiable desires can lead to various attachments, compulsions, and addictions that lead to suffering.

Teaching: Rituals of Survival

Willy is the soft, hungry, child exiled to the closet, and he is also the part of us who sneaks, hides, and numbs so no one has to see that pain. In the language of Internal Family Systems (IFS), he spans both inner worlds: the raw exile carrying the weight of early shame and the clever protector who emerged to keep that shame tucked away, untouched. He developed rituals, not to defy, but to survive. In the dark, in the quiet, in the body, he found ways to soothe the hunger that no one else seemed to see.

And society?

It doesn't just ignore the closet. It helps build it. It hands boys a blueprint of stoicism and scorn. Do not be sensitive. It whispers loudly that vulnerability is weakness, and that tenderness is a threat. It makes hunger, whether for food, touch, or love, a flaw, something to be masked or managed. Nourishment becomes a performance. Appetite becomes guilt. We are taught that real men don't cry, don't eat too much, don't get soft, don't touch themselves, and certainly don't ask for more, more connection, affection, and truth.

And in that silence, many turn to secret rituals, to screens, fantasies, performances of control, to manage what was never allowed to be felt. The isolation of porn addiction isn't about pleasure. It's about loneliness. About needing to feel *something* in a world that taught you to feel *nothing*. We will cover this further in chapter 7, where the digital field becomes both a mirror and a maze.

But what if we did?

What if we listened to the exiled protector parts like Willy, not to silence them, but to honor their brilliance and resilience? What if strength wasn't the ability to suppress hunger but the courage to feel it fully and feed it wisely?

To welcome the hunger is to welcome the child. Not to shame it. But to seat it at the table, again. When that happens, we are able to embrace the soft parts, to laugh, to sing and to have joy.

For some of us, feeding ourselves with kindness is more than an act of nourishment, it's an act of defiance. Because beneath the hunger for food, or care, or recognition, lies another kind of hunger. One we often carry in silence. A hunger shaped by harm. For those whose bodies became battlegrounds before they became homes, the journey toward nourishment is not just about what we eat, it's about what we survived. And sometimes, the body remembers what the mind cannot say.

Teaching: Recognition as Nourishment

Hunger comes in many forms, and often, the deepest hunger is not for food but for recognition, for someone to look at us with presence and kindness and say, "I see you. You matter."

As children, we weren't just hungry for sandwiches or sweets. We were hungry to be understood, to be held in a gaze that didn't flinch, to be mirrored and acknowledged, not for what we did, but for who we were. When that didn't come, we turned to what was available. Food became a stand-in for affection, a surrogate for attention, a loyal companion that didn't ask questions or look away.

In many ways, we were asking the world, "Can you see me?" But no one knew how to answer, so we answered ourselves with mouthfuls of something sweet, soft, and numbing, the kind of quiet fullness that made the ache of invisibility briefly disappear.

Psychologists and neuroscientists now tell us that being seen, heard, and co-regulated, especially in childhood, is foundational to emotional health. Recognition is not a luxury; it is a form of psychic nutrition. Without it, the soul grows gaunt, the body finds other ways to cope, and the hunger never truly goes away.

Today, we know that recognition is a sacred act. To look at a child, or at any part of ourselves, and say, "I see you. You don't have to hide anymore," is a kind of feeding. It satisfies something deeper than appetite; it speaks to our being.

If we were never seen as children, we need to hear this now: we deserved to be, and we still do. It is never too late to feed that part of us with the gift of attention, compassion, and care.

Food was never the problem. Neither was desire. The real wound was shame, an inherited, internalized belief that certain parts were too much, too needy, too soft, too hungry to be worthy of love. It was the shame of simply being in one's skin.

Willy didn't emerge from brokenness. He emerged from a primal need to stay alive, and also from fear. He arrived to help navigate the unbearable. To be there when no one else was. To offer pleasure when the world demanded performance. To give a sense of control when everything else felt chaotic.

For years, we may have believed that we had to earn our place at the table, by shrinking, by striving, by pretending we were not starving. But now we understand: the table was never meant to exclude the parts of us that were still learning how to speak, feel, and receive.

To integrate Willy, or that part of ourselves that has been hidden, we must not silence them but invite them home. Not to discipline them, but to **dialogue** with them. It is to realize that the voice of hunger is also the voice of wisdom, it tells us where we are empty, what we truly long for, and what we were once denied.

> **PRACTICE & REFLECTION:**
> **From Coping to Consciousness**
>
> When we move from **coping** to **consciously relating** with our parts, the protectors and exiles, something profound happens, we reclaim our sovereignty. We stop managing symptoms and start nurturing wholeness.
>
> **Sovereignty is not perfection.**
>
> It is presence.
> It is the right to exist without apology.
> It is the decision to stop outsourcing our worth to others.
> It is feeding the Self we once starved.
>
> **Ask Yourself**
>
> *Where in my life am I still trying to "earn" my right to eat, to rest, to receive?*
>
> *What part of me still believes I have to hide my appetite, whether physical, emotional, or sexual?*
>
> *How do I treat myself when I feel "too much"? With shame, or with space?*
>
> *What would it mean to live without secrecy?*
>
> **Use an Affirmation**
>
> *I am no longer starving.*
> *I welcome all parts of myself to the table.*
> *I choose food, touch, and truth that nourish, not numb.*
> *My hunger is not a weakness, it is a compass pointing me home.*

Breathe In. Breathe Out.

Follow Your Spirit. Follow Your Heart.

The Inner Sanctuary

*"Beneath the noise and battle lies a still place.
The sanctuary is not found, it is remembered within breath,
within body, within heart."*

— Keith W. Fiveson

Chapter 5:
Dreams, Nightmares, and Breathing

👣 Story: The Dragon and Messages

Willy was six years old when the dragon swooped in to take him. Not a fairy tale dragon, but one made of fire and feathers, ancient and terrible. It was like a Phoenix, swooping down with wings and screams to claim him, not once, but again and again, night after night, hunting, not just him, but some vulnerable essence of him. Willy. The soft boy who had not yet armored up. He still believed that life was safe.

Years later, during therapy and in Al-Anon recovery, he returned to these dreams not to analyze them, but to listen. He began to ask: What if the dragon wasn't just the threat? What if it was also the messenger? The dragon's transformation into figures of authority and pursuit, soldiers, police, men armed with weapons, signaled a shift in the narrative of the dream. Willy's fantastical threat morphed into a harsh reality that mirrored his life on the streets. The constant chase, the desperate need to evade and survive; it's what hardened him. It was within these dreams that Jason, the Numb Armor, who was not afraid to run away, would emerge.

Jason embodied the survival instincts that Willy had developed. He was the runner, the vigilant, the one who could not afford to show fear. This was the beginning stages of another protective shell, a persona that would eventually crystallize into the fully formed archetype, often rebellious Jason. But Jason didn't just form to protect Willy in dreams, he grew up with him. He graduated, got older, and moved out of the basement. He got his own suits. His own office. His own list of rules.

Jason learned to use silence like a weapon. To walk into a room and own it, not through authenticity, but through precision. Sex, drugs, quarterly bonuses, he excelled at all of them. He married twice. Demolished both. Not out of malice, but from the sheer inability to stay present, to stay soft. To be in relationship you needed to be vulnerable, and he didn't want that.

Jason wasn't broken. He was brilliant.

He was also haunted.

Behind the crisp shirts, suits, and expense accounts, he was still the boy checking exits, still the runner. Still, the dreamer who learned early that sleep was dangerous, rest was a luxury, and vulnerability was a liability.

He worked so hard to become the dragon-slayer that he didn't notice when he became the dragon himself.

Two marriages, success and debauchery in the corporate world, a life full of cash and prizes, but peace of mind? That was nowhere to be found.

And Jason knew it. He just didn't know what to do with it. Not yet.

Jason had mastered the art of survival. He'd learned to read people, seal deals, charm partners, and crush competitors. But he had never learned how to sit still. He never learned how to breathe into his own emptiness.

The armor wasn't just physical, it was existential. A personality built on prevention: prevent pain, prevent closeness, prevent failure. And for a long time, it worked. Until it didn't. Nights grew longer. The wins felt hollow. The applause faded faster. The mirror became harder to look into, not because of

aging, but because of the absence in his own eyes. The shadow wasn't just around him. It *was* him. The part he refused to grieve. The dragon he stopped running from . . . and started embodying.

Jason did not know how to stop. Stopping would mean facing what the dragon had whispered all along, that he was not broken, only burdened. That the armor was never his true skin. That sleep, deep restorative sleep, was not weakness but surrender. He feared surrender most of all because it threatened his illusion of control.

But there were signs, cracks in the steel. A second divorce he didn't see coming. A panic attack before a presentation. A dream of a boy in a closet, silent and small, whispering through the static of his breath. Jason was still running, but his legs were tired. The shadow wasn't chasing anymore. It was waiting. Waiting for him to stop. To turn. To face it, not as an enemy, but as a guide.

Jason's hardened exterior was forged in the fires of adversity. Willy's dreams were not just a reflection of his reality; they were the crucible in which his protective persona was formed. The evolution of his dreams and the emergence of Jason were inextricably linked, a testament to the mind's power to adapt and survive in the face of overwhelming hardship.

But not all dreams were filled with fear. In time, other dreams emerged, softer, gentler visions that arrived like gifts. Dreams where Willy floated in water warmed by sunlight, or curled in a large blanket beside a flickering fire. In these dreams, no one was chasing. He was being held. Safe. The child in him, so often forgotten, was finally being seen, felt, and loved.

These good dreams, though rare, became nourishment. They reminded him of what he was yearning for: rest, restoration, and relationship. The importance of feeling held, caressed, and deeply known. In those moments, he remembered what it was like to be in touch with touch. To feel safe enough to sleep. Safe enough to dream.

👣 Story: The Trip That Changed the Map

When the noise began to quiet, after the second divorce, the panic attack, the dreams where he was finally held, something softer began to rise. Beneath the strategies and suits, before the armor fused to his skin, there was a different time. A memory that didn't roar but whispered.

It was before Jason learned to suit up, show up, and shut down. Before Willy found fleeting sanctuary in dreams. A window of time when neither boy had yet hardened. When fear hadn't fully taken the wheel. They hadn't yet learned the rules of survival, hadn't yet built walls high enough to keep out pain, or high enough to block connection.

There was a trip, unremarkable to most, but unforgettable to them. A moment when the map hadn't yet been drawn in bold lines of defense. A glimpse of what it felt like to simply be: unguarded, undefined, and still becoming.

While Timothy Leary sat in solitary confinement at Folsom Prison, his psychedelic revolution dissolving under the weight of punishment and politics, Willy was walking his own edge. He wasn't leading a movement. He was trying to understand the pain he carried. Psychedelic Medicine (LSD, mushrooms) and Breathwork. Each one opened a doorway. He didn't always find clarity, but sometimes something beyond the noise emerged, a memory, a message, a truth too long buried. Dreams became lucid. Emotions surfaced raw. He remembered. What was lost was found. Once, he wept at the sight of a spiderweb, its glistening threads revealing a world bound by beauty and breath, interconnected, like Indra's web.

What began as personal exploration slowly deepened into something more intentional. He learned the difference between escape and return. He began to understand the power of preparation, of sacred space, of being held in community. He sat in circles with others, not just to journey, but to heal. Integration became the real work. They shared stories. Faced shadows. Tended

wounds. Together, they created a field where something ancient stirred, a way of remembering that we are not alone, and never were.

In one non-ordinary state, he saw himself falling upward, past planets, past ancestors, past the body he had once trusted. He didn't feel called to God. He felt unmoored. Untethered, a part of a Universal Cosmic Goo, like a raindrop, a spec light, a dot in God's creation, connected to everything and nothing but presence and pure potential.

The commune was a cocoon, but it was not a container. It was time to choose the ground again, to "Ramble on." Not to float, but to land. Not to escape, but to endure. He didn't know it then, but the psychedelic openings had only cleared the debris. What came next required structure, bone, oath, uniform.

Willy couldn't have named what was happening, only that something in him was trying to heal. The "medicine" showed him how beauty could shatter him open. How pain could dissolve into stars. For a while, it worked. The boundaries fell away, and he felt part of everything. But without grounding, the awe turned unstable. What was sacred became unspeakable, and eventually, unbearable.

That's when Willy realized: to survive this world, he would need more than visions. He needed something stronger, like boundaries and distance. Orders. Edges. Something solid.

So, one day, he left. Walked out barefoot and thumbed a ride into town. And he joined the Army.

People thought it made no sense. But to Willy, it made perfect sense. The Army was the promise of a bigger community, a rhythm he could follow. He needed gravity. He needed rules. He needed to find a way to sleep without "floating off the earth."

That was the day Jason showed up, not just as a protector, but as a strategist. Not as a boy in a blanket, but as a man in a uniform. But Jason didn't make the plan alone. As Willy stood between the chaos of dreams and the certainty of

the recruiter's office, something colder stirred. A calculation. A part that didn't flinch, didn't feel, only planned.

"Follow orders. Learn the rules. Play the game. Survive."

It wasn't courage. It was calculus. It was survival repackaged as ambition. On that day, without knowing it, Willy birthed two protectors:

Jason, who would run faster, and Tom, who would outthink danger before it arrived.

These parts, together, would build a life that looked strong. But somewhere, beneath the uniforms, promotions, and marriages, the Exiled Child still dreamed of something softer. He just didn't know how to find it yet. It wasn't a betrayal. It was survival. He needed to pick a role. So, he did.

And in sleep, the body remembered. The dreams, chaotic or calm, were never just stories. They were signals and emotional truths that had nowhere else to go. That's where the real work began.

🪶 Teaching: IFS Insight, Dreams

Dreams are not meaningless echoes of the day's events. They are encoded messages from the unconscious, revealing truths we may not be ready to face in daylight. In trauma-informed frameworks such as Jungian psychology and Internal Family Systems (IFS), dreams serve as symbolic arenas where *exiled parts* surface, not to torment us, but to be *witnessed*.

The dragon that haunted Willy was more than a predator, it symbolized the fire of transformation. In myth, dragons are not simply destroyers; they are often guardians of treasure. Similarly, the Phoenix rises from ashes, signifying renewal. These motifs point to a universal truth: the treasure lies on the other side of fear. In dreamwork, that treasure is the insight we gain by confronting what we would rather avoid.

The soldiers and police in dreams, those uniformed, nameless, faceless pursuers, often represent internalized authority figures, the rigid protectors of

the psyche's established order. These are the inner critics and managers that IFS identifies as survival parts. Jason, as an archetype, was shaped in response to such threats. He is the armored tactician, the one who ensures we stay ahead of pain. But survival has a cost. Jason cannot rest. He cannot sleep deeply. Over time, the dreamscape becomes not a sanctuary, but a battleground.

Trauma survivors often misinterpret dreams as signs of relapse or failure. In reality, dreams are the soul's rehearsal space, a private theater where exiled parts attempt to reenact pain not to perpetuate it, but to *complete it*. These dreamscapes serve as test flights for integration, where the dragon transforms from enemy to emissary, and running gives way to remembering.

Teaching: Breath to Self-Regulate

In trauma recovery, regulating the nervous system is not optional, but it is essential if we are to be in the "Window of Tolerance." So, practices like yoga, massage, and conscious breathwork such as box breathing, or the 4-7-8 technique are more than coping mechanisms. They are essential disciplines of self-regulation, trusted by elite performers, combat veterans, and survivors of deep emotional wounding. These methods help maintain composure in high-stress environments, bridging the gap between inner chaos and outer functioning.

Breath, when used intentionally, becomes a stabilizing force. Not to armor oneself, but to anchor. When paced and conscious, it sends signals to the body that it is safe enough to release hypervigilance and allow rest. The exhale becomes a permission slip to soften.

At a certain stage of healing, another shift becomes possible, not through effort, but through allowance. This shift is not about doing more, but about letting go. Instead of aversion, we seek acceptance. When striving ceases, the body may begin to access a deeper, parasympathetic state. This is a physiological reset where the nervous system shifts from fight-or-flight into restoration and repair.

In this space, connection is reestablished. Touch can be received as comfort rather than threat. Stillness can be felt not as danger, but as sanctuary. The body begins to remember the pleasure of breath at rest, the feeling of limbs growing heavy under the weight of trust, the safety of simply being held.

In a culture that worships productivity and numbs discomfort, rest becomes countercultural. It is not regression, it is remembrance. A return to a fundamental truth that healing does not always come through action. Sometimes, it comes through surrender.

During deep sleep, the immune system is strengthened. Emotional memories are consolidated. The dreaming mind becomes a messenger for what words cannot yet speak. Good dreams reconnect us to a state of wholeness we may have forgotten, but never truly lost.

Rest is not a reward. It is a return. A place where the Exiled Child within us no longer needs to run, but is welcomed home, not in defeat, but in belonging.

Teaching-Reflection: Examine Dreams for Mythical Truths

To work with dreams is to work with the subconscious theater of the Exiled Child. Nightmares are not signs of dysfunction-they are invitations to integrate. Every time we listen, record, breathe, and reflect, we reclaim a part of ourselves that was once lost at night.

Good dreams are just as important as the frightening ones. They carry medicine, too. They remind us of what's possible when we are no longer at war with ourselves. When we allow ourselves to be held, softened, and sleep deeply enough to return to the places where we were once whole, ***sometimes it requires that we lay ourselves onto the altar to be altered.*** And sometimes, when the dreaming is done, we wake to find something waiting within us, not a protector, not a pursuer, but a presence.

The **Golden Child** is not the boy who ran, or the man or woman that strategized. The part of us that remembered who we were *meant* to become. Not perfect. Not polished. But possible. The part of us that carries the **aspiration** of wholeness, not just success, but **integrity**.

A good conscience. A quiet heart. The kind of inner peace that lets you rest easy. Because a good night's sleep is not just about melatonin or meditation, it's about **living in alignment**. It's about not having to run anymore. We often think awakening requires effort. But the real threshold is surrender. Sometimes, the key to the door isn't force, it's **acceptance**. And sometimes, the altar we seek is not out there, but *within*. The place we lay our restless selves down and say:

"Enough. I'm ready to stop performing. I'm ready to come home."

That's when the Golden Child rises. Not to save us. But to remind us that we were always whole. We just needed to sleep deeply enough . . . to remember.

This chapter closes not with a technique, but with a truth: what chases you in dreams may one day become your teacher. And what cradles you in dreams may one day become your healer.

Sleep is not a shutdown, it's a sacred shift. A recalibration of the nervous system, a return to coherence. When we meet our dreams with presence, we are no longer just resting. We are reassembling, not into the selves we were told to become, but into the truth of the Self we've always carried within.

| Practice & Reflection: **Meeting the Dream** |

1. **Bedtime Ritual**: Set a simple intention before you go to sleep. Whisper, "May I remember what seeks to be healed tonight?"
2. **Dream Dialogue**: Keep a notebook or voice recorder by your bed. Upon waking, write down or record anything you remember, even fragments.
3. **Archetype Reflection**: Ask yourself: Who appeared in the dream? What did they want? What part of me do they represent?
4. **Guided Inquiry**:
   - What is the dragon trying to protect me from?
   - If your exiled protector showed up, what was he doing, running, fighting, or hiding?
   - What does the dream want me to feel?
5. **Body Integration**: After a strong dream, place a hand on your chest or belly. Breathe deeply. Ground the dream in your body.

> **PRACTICE: RECONNECTING WITH SAFE TOUCH**
>
> - Wrap yourself in a blanket or hold a pillow as if you are being held.
> - Recall a memory or image of being lovingly touched by a parent, pet, or even a dream figure.
> - Say to yourself: "It's okay to rest now. I am safe."

> **PRACTICE: RECONNECTING WITH SAFE TOUCH**
>
> Stand in front of a mirror. Look into your own eyes. Don't perform. Don't critique, just witness.

Breathe deeply.

Say aloud:

**"I see the parts of me I've tried to outgrow.
The parts that fought, seduced, and succeeded.
I thank them.
And I ask now for something more honest.
Not perfect. But present."**

Let the breath guide you, not toward fixing, but toward *facing*.

CHAPTER 6:
Relationships, The Golden Child

👣 Story: Love That Was Too Much and Never Enough

Willy grew up surrounded by people who shared his blood but not his home. He was an only child in a fragmented family constellation, a single star in a broken sky. His mother married three times, his father five. He had five half-brothers and two half-sisters, but none of them grew up with him. They were echoes, not companions.

In families like Willy's, silence becomes its own inheritance. The siblings spun in disconnected orbits, each shaped by a different version of truth, time, and abandonment. Though they shared blood, they had not shared belonging. In constellations like these, love often resembles distance, present, but unreachable.

Steele, the eldest of Willy's half-brothers, stood out in the constellation like a charismatic cipher. He was successful in many visible ways, accomplished, sharp, and socially agile, but carried an unnamed sorrow that lived just beneath the surface. Short in stature but fast in speech, Steele's intelligence often arrived wrapped in cutting humor. His tongue was precise, his sarcasm reflexive. Affection, when offered, was rarely clean. A compliment came with a jab. Intimacy came with withdrawal.

Willy admired him and feared him in equal measure. Steele had learned from their father that love was conditional, and he played the role well, offering warmth as long as performance continued. Approval was possible, but always earned. Connection, if it came, was temporary.

Interlude, The Brother Beyond Reach

There are wounds that never bleed, just quietly burn beneath the skin. For Willy, Steele was one of them.

Years after their father died, Steele reached out, saying he had questions. But the questions weren't just about facts, they were layered with grief, unspoken feelings, and decades of estrangement. Willy tried to make space, but the moment dissolved quickly. The tone turned sharp. Old shadows took the lead. Words flared. Then silence.

Steele accused. Willy reacted. The wall of armor rose.

Later, Willy reached out to mend the break, acknowledging his part. Steele replied, "You've never really liked me. That's the pattern. I'll always care that you're well, but anything else is beyond my reach."

That phrase echoed in Willy's mind: *beyond my reach*.

Perhaps they had always been too far apart. Perhaps the father wound cut them both differently. Steele's exile had its own shape, formed not just by geography, but by pride, pain, and disillusionment. Willy no longer chased connections that wouldn't come. But he did grieve the loss, not just of the brother he barely had, but of the relationship he once imagined they could have.

Not all connections were like Steele's. Later in life, Willy would meet people who offered warmth without condition, friends who called just to listen, mentors who encouraged without strings attached. These relationships

didn't erase the ache for his brother, but they reminded him that connection could be simple, even healing.

Archetype Reflection: The Shadow Brother

In families fractured by betrayal or neglect, there is often a sibling who becomes more than a person, they become a symbol. For Willy, Steele was the *Shadow Brother*: brilliant, cutting, distant, and unreachable. He mirrored the parts of Willy still desperate for paternal approval, still afraid of rejection, still longing for recognition. Steele's sarcasm wasn't just communication, it was a wall. A defense. A flare of pain.

This archetype appears in many lives: a brother, friend, colleague, or partner who always seems to stand one rung above, looking down. The Shadow Brother teaches us where our own shame still lives, and where we must stop handing over the keys to our peace.

Not all estrangements are born in adulthood. The ache for brotherhood, recognition, understanding, kinship, ran like a river through Willy's life. Steele wasn't the first, and wouldn't be the last to leave him reaching across in silence. Long before that exchange, another brother had entered the picture, one whose presence awakened both hope and hesitation.

When Kerk, another older half-brother, entered Willy's life at the age of seven, it felt like a bridge was finally being built. Kerk, born from the hidden relationship between Willy's mother and her mother's boyfriend, carried a legacy laced with secrecy and shame. Still, he brought a different kind of energy, less sharp, more present. Willy, young and eager for connection, welcomed the possibility of brotherhood, unaware of the undercurrents of unresolved damage flowing just beneath their early bond.

Years later, in his late twenties and newly divorced, Willy was trying to maintain a fragile thread of stability for his young son. His ex-wife still carried his last name. Their child did too. It wasn't perfect, but it was intact. But even fragile things can be broken.

Kerk began appearing more often. At first, it looked like support, family stepping in to help hold the pieces together. Willy welcomed it cautiously. After all, real connection had been rare, and part of him still longed for someone to show up, to prove that not all family ties were conditional.

But then, something changed.

The rhythm of care became less steady. There were pauses where connection used to be, absences where trust once stood. Conversations that once felt open now carried a weight, something unspoken just beneath the surface.

And then came the truth. Kerk was dating Willy's soon to be ex-wife. There had been no discussion. No explanation. Just silence followed by certainty. Eventually, they married.

Willy shut down. Jason stepped in, and numbness became the only strategy. The weekend visits with his son became rituals of restraint, no softness, no play. Suspicion edged every exchange. His protector Tom tried to organize it, to make meaning of what had no logic. His manager, Sarah, tried to smooth it over. But nothing helped. The parts did what they could, and still, something in him pulled away.

For over three decades, Willy and Kerk didn't speak. No calls. No acknowledgment. The silence hardened into a boundary, then into habit. The betrayal lived on, not just as memory, but as absence.

And then, near the end, the phone rang. Kerk was preparing for a second heart surgery. His voice was quiet. Apologetic. He said he knew what he'd done. That it had hurt. He asked for forgiveness. Willy listened. The parts were all there, Jason guarded, Tom reserved, Sarah already leaning forward. It wasn't easy. But it was real.

They met once, face to face. It was tentative, unfinished, but honest. The bridge had broken long ago, but for a moment, the two stood where it once had been. Some sweet moments ensued, but nothing could heal what was taken away.

Kerk died four years later.

The wound didn't vanish. But it changed shape. It had been named. Witnessed. The silence was broken. And something in Willy exhaled.

In other places of his life, repair looked different. It came in shared coffee with a 12-step group, in quiet talks with an old friend after years of misunderstanding, or in a simple hug from a colleague when words failed. Not every rupture needed to end in distance or silence. Sometimes, showing up imperfectly was enough.

When people asked how he kept going, he would often think of the words Leonard Cohen wrote: *"Ring the bells that still can ring, forget your perfect offering. There is a crack in everything, that's how the light gets in."*

Even so, for Willy, love was not always a sanctuary. It was often a source of anxiety and hidden pain. His experiences taught him that those who offered affection could also inflict harm or leave without warning. This fear became the bedrock of his anxious attachment, marked by a constant need for reassurance and the ache that closeness might slip away at any moment. Like his dreams, he was always hiding or running in his relationships. Sometimes this looked like clinging or jealousy, sometimes a quiet withdrawal when he felt too exposed.

He learned how to be interdependent, with his caretaker protector always ready to fill the gaps.

Healing begins when we cut the cords of betrayal and anchor ourselves in a deeper field of belonging. Our relationships are not just memories; they are living entanglements, threads spun through generations. Healing them is not about forgetting, but about transforming how we hold them inside us. It is through this transformation that we reconnect to our Core Self, the center of dignity, resilience, and love that was never truly lost.

Story: Managers and Protectors, Forged in Military Uniform

At one point in this life, Willy was an army corporal, stationed in West Germany in the mid-70s, living in close quarters with men who rotated in and out of his life like the cold winter, snow, and wind through the Bavarian barracks. It was still the Cold War back then, and he learned German in Munich and perfected the art of disappearing into the culture, learning to fit in, look busy, dress sharp, obey orders, stay silent, and avoid any conversations that veered toward family, future, or feelings. He always kept to himself.

Back then, Jason, the protector, was running the show. He was the one selling liquor and cigarettes to the German civilians and heading to France to be the "ringer" at a carnival boxing fight-show, or randomly sleeping with gypsies, and later bragging about it. He was the wild one. His protector, Tom, was emerging as a top-secret encoder and decoder. There was a staff sergeant who once called Willy over and asked, "You ever miss home?" Willy didn't flinch. "Not really." The sergeant nodded, and smiled, like he'd heard it before.

Willy was living his life, learning, loving, and saving for an uncertain future. He got back in touch with his mother back then. It was awkward, strange and yet he was curious as to who this woman was. She once sent him

a gift box from Brooklyn, which took a month to get there and was spoiled rotten by the time it arrived. It was sweet, but really said it all. The package was too late, spoiled, and had to be thrown away. He laughed and chalked it up to the alcohol and just not thinking clearly.

Tom, the strategist, was always calculating, distanced, disciplined, and hypervigilant. He learned quickly, planned meticulously, and anticipated each step of the day with a quiet precision, scanning for threats before they had form. He was determined to keep moving away from the chaos of his origins, toward something orderly, earned, and safe. By twenty-two, Tom the protector had nudged Willy into a disciplined Army life and enrollment in Heidelberg University, where military service ran parallel with academic rigor. He learned German and got promoted to assist the post commander, a trusted, punctual, and exacting position. His clearance was top secret. His desk was measured to perfection, everything aligned to the millimeter. In Tom's world, control equaled safety. He wore stoicism like a pressed uniform: clean lines, no creases, no emotion, extra starch. He didn't fumble or flinch. His friendships were efficient, not intimate. His calendar overflowed, yet his gut remained clenched, his boots shined to a mirrored gloss. He could brief the colonel without blinking but couldn't name the hollow ache that crept in on Sunday nights, when the quiet settled. The dreams always came, figures of command and punishment, dragons in uniform, authority with a weapon drawn.

The watcher, Mr. Moto, silently guided, breath by breath, listening to the silence beneath the structure, being there when Willy would stop managing his life and start living and being it. To be as a human being. But even in those tightly packed days, where every move was timed, every emotion rationed, Mr. Moto formed his own quiet ranks. In moments when Willy stood rigid during inspections or recited regulations under a commander's narrowed gaze, breath became the hidden formation behind the posture. Inhale for four. Hold. Exhale for four.

Willy's life also required great care and it was his protector and manager Sarah, the Caregiver archetype Willy's protector, managing through care, cleaning, and self-preservation, who showed up to nurture and protect him, to wash, brush and clean the old and make way for the new. Sarah was about self-preservation and care, the only safe language.

Sarah was also quite the performer, lighting up several productions staged for Army service members through the Morale, Welfare, and Recreation (MWR) program. But her relationship with the stage went deeper than

morale-boosting entertainment. Before the uniforms and inspections, before the barracks and bunk beds, Sarah had studied with legends Lee Strasberg and Stella Adler during her tempestuous youth. Back then, she had been "acting out" in every sense of the word, and acting became her sanctuary. The stage gave her voice, shape, and fire. She carried that training like a hidden compass, even when life pulled her far from its creative North.

On base, her charisma still shone. Her performances were tight, captivating, precise. But the limited creative outlets left her restless. So, she picked up a secondhand camera and began capturing portraits, fellow service members caught in tender, unguarded moments. She sold the photos across the base, her art quietly circulating, offering beauty in a place built for function.

In the barracks, Sarah brought that same discipline and care to everything she touched. Her bunk was tight. Hospital corners exact. Boots and buckles gleamed. Shirts weren't just ironed; they were curated. Her hands were always in motion, folding, stitching, polishing, part ritual, part resistance. A way to keep the heart from breaking. She carried grace like armor. Creativity like a buried ember. And somewhere deep inside, she still hoped that love, or something like it, might rediscover her, not just as the caretaker, but as the artist she had always been. Sometimes, in the quiet just before lights-out, Sarah would sit on the edge of the bunk, staring at the creases in the blanket like they were lines in a script. In those moments, the voices of her old teachers would resurface.

"Don't act the emotion," Stella had told her, eyes sharp as glass. "Find the truth underneath it. That's where the soul of the scene lives."

Lee had spoken of the *private moment,* the unscripted space where something real breaks through.

Sarah used to chase those moments like oxygen. She remembered the trembling stillness of the stage, the power of silence, the electricity of being seen. Back then, it felt like transformation was possible, like becoming someone else might finally make her feel like herself.

Now, her performances took place in fluorescent-lit hallways and tightly tucked hospital corners. She wasn't the clever, pretty one anymore, she was the director behind the scenes, cueing lines, smoothing wrinkles, managing appearances. She kept Willy composed and clean, safe, tempered, and prepared. It was her duty and her devotion. But the stage had never left her. Even now, folding linens or aligning locker doors, she felt her fingers mimic

the gestures of a curtain call. Not for praise. But for release. For the quiet recognition that she still mattered, not just as caretaker, but as soul.

But sometimes, in the quiet, she imagined stepping back onto the stage, not to play a role, but to reclaim her own voice. Not for applause, but to remember she still had one saying . . .

> "You are not just the role you play.
>
> You are the life beneath it.
>
> Breathe. You are made of stars."

Teaching: Entanglements Across Time

Years after the Army, Willy looked back and saw that much of his emotional upheaval stemmed from more than his own past. It was a quantum entanglement: unseen threads of pain, betrayal, and the will to survive, spanning generations and resonating with unresolved grief, depression, addiction, suicide, and shattered connections across diverse backgrounds.

For many of us, these patterns extend beyond individual lives and families within our broader society. Trauma's impact radiates outward, embedded in actions, unspoken words, and the very atmosphere connecting us all, regardless of origin or identity. Eventually, Willy would learn that healing involved not only his own freedom but also recognizing and unraveling these inherited influences to select a different resonance, a new inclusive narrative.

Teaching-Story: Wounds and Reclamation

Willy, now much older, found himself still affected by his past. He was happy with his third wife, ready to enjoy time away, when a text message came in from his brother. Steele could instantly provoke a strong negative response: a constricted chest, a surge of adrenaline, and a wave of shame. He recalled Steele's lengthy text messages filled with sharp insults, sarcasm, bombastic language, and name-calling, because Willy couldn't accommodate an unexpected arrival, with him, his new bride, and a stepson, when he was heading out of town. Steele would belittle Willy's achievements and depreciate his masculinity. He even resorted to insulting Willy's wife after she confronted him about inappropriate behavior.

During these periods of confrontation, Willy's internal protectors scrambled into formation, Jason preparing to cut ties, Tom started constructing defensive

arguments, and Sarah prayed for kindness and reconciliation. Beneath them, the Exiled Child braced for another unseen blow.

But this time, with Mr. Moto's breath-walk guidance, Willy stopped, took a breath, and noticed. He placed a hand lightly over his chest, feeling the steady rhythm of his heart. He breathed deeply into his belly, the way Mr. Moto had taught him, rooting himself in the now.

> *"This is not my storm,"* he whispered to the frightened parts inside.
> *"We don't have to sail into it."*

With that breath, Willy stepped out of the battle. He chose to respond, not with anger, not with explanation, not with self-defense. He chose silence. He chose peace. He chose compassion. And in that small, invisible act, he reclaimed his dignity.

> *Healing doesn't always begin with forgiveness. Sometimes it starts with the courage not to reenact the old scene. To step out of the loop, not in vengeance but in peace. To say "We're done rehearsing this script. I'm rewriting the role I play."*

꧁ Teaching-Story: Reclaiming Our Ancestors

Rewriting the script, changing roles, and bringing the council of parts together, is essential. Willy had used non-ordinary states of consciousness, enabled through holotropic breathwork sessions to break through the wall of armor surrounding his ego in order to accept himself and all the parts and ancestors of transgenerational trauma.

During one session, Willy went very deep with his breath rising like a tide, falling like a drumbeat. Again, and again, deep breathing. He lay on the mat in the center of a breathwork circle, eyes closed, the music pulsing around him like waves on the shore. As the rhythm built, his body began to tense, and shake, not in fear, but in release. In this opening, his mind connected with a visual of something ancient.

The Ancestors

They stood not on the earth, but in the sky, above and behind him, a living constellation. He recognized no faces, but he felt their presence in his bones, the way a son knows the scent of his mother's skin, or the rhythm of his

grandfather's walk. They were from both mother and father, very old generations that suffered. He felt and saw them in his whole body, visceral and real, like the DNA and blood flowing through his skin, a heartbeat, or a breath. They were looking at him. Smiling, they were not judging, or even watching. They were witnessing him.

We see you, they whispered. *You have carried us. We are proud of you.*

The words weren't spoken but vibrated. He heard them. His throat clenched and tears rolled down both cheeks. All the parts of him, the numb child, the strategic man, the armored one, melted into stillness. In their place stood the boy he had hidden for decades. Barefoot. Breathing. Glowing.

The exile is over, the wind seemed to say. *You belong to yourself now.*

When Willy opened his eyes, the room was unchanged. But inside, the fracture had closed. Not perfectly. Not forever. But enough.

Cutting the Thread: Reclaiming the Golden Child

Forgiveness was never about erasing what happened. It was about refusing to let the past dictate the future. Willy could bless those who had wounded him without inviting them back into his sacred space. It was a "friendly boundary" designed to keep him safe and at peace and those that were mindless far away from him.

In choosing presence over reactivity, he exalted the Exiled Child within, not into naïve vulnerability, but into sovereign strength. He honored the part of himself that had survived, that had loved, that had endured. He activated the Golden Child not as a role to be earned, but as an essence to be lived. The Golden Child was not naïve. He was luminous, resilient, and wise. His light was not born of innocence alone, but of survival, forgiveness, and the radical choice to trust life again. The Golden Child carried joy, curiosity, and the sacred belief that he belonged, not because he earned it, but because he always had. He became his own safe sanctuary.

The Golden Child within us is the undimmed spark that persists beyond all betrayals. It is the part of us that still dares to dream, to play, to love freely. Reclaiming the Golden Child is not about becoming someone new; it is about remembering who we were before we forgot. It is about weaving together our wisdom, our pain, and our unbreakable spirit into a new kind of wholeness.

The Journey Back to the Golden Child, the Core Self.

Across world mythologies, this is the path of exile and return, the descent into fragmentation and the climb back toward wholeness. In the monomyth, it is the return phase, not with spoils or triumph, but with integration. The child is not restored through conquest, but through remembrance.

This journey is rarely a straight line. It unfolds in spirals and stumbles, in tremors rather than declarations. The Golden Child does not return with fanfare, but in small ruptures, a laugh that feels too loud, a tear shed too easily, a moment of trust offered too soon. Sometimes it feels foolish. Sometimes it feels like a risk. But when these signals are welcomed, not judged or shamed, something ancient begins to breathe again.

The exile ends not with a performance, but with a pause. Not with certainty, but with breath. With the Core Self whispering, 'You are not a role. You are not a failure. You belong.' The Self, the calm, curious, and clear, was never gone. It waited behind the noise, behind the shame. This is the universal pilgrimage: exile, descent, and return. Myth remembers it as the Hero's Journey, indigenous traditions as the spirit child recalled from dreamtime, scripture as the prodigal son embraced, not for perfection, but for being always beloved.

Exercise: Honoring the Exiled Child

- What relationships in your life still activate old survival patterns?
- What would it mean to bless those connections, not by inviting harm, but by releasing their hold on you?
- Where does the Exiled Child within you still wait to be seen, held, protected?
- How might the Core Self within you call your Golden Child back into belonging?

Teaching: Asking for what's needed

When we don't know what we need, want, or we're afraid to ask for it, others won't know how to help, be present, or show up for you. This can happen. A first experience with divorce, death, vitality, cognitive function, etc., can be overwhelming, and learning how to ask for what we need can stem from trust issues developed early in life. These patterns can lead to the exile of those vulnerable parts of ourselves, protected by a complex system of internal "protectors" that prevent us from expressing our actual needs, out of fear of rejection or harm. We might live in a world of "ifs," *if* I ask, I'll be a burden; *if* I show vulnerability, I'll be abandoned. Thus, we create the causes and conditions that validate and reaffirm our self-doubts.

Creating a "safe container" within relationships is crucial for dismantling these protective barriers and allowing our exiled parts to emerge. This safety is built upon clearly defined oaths, mutual rules, and healthy boundaries, fostering clear communication. These structures provide predictability and trust, assuring us that our vulnerability will be met with respect and care, not judgment or exploitation. When such a container exists, we feel safer identifying and articulating our needs, fostering deeper connections, and healing the wounds of faulty attachments. Without clear communication, misunderstandings can arise; we might say, "I heard what you said, but I didn't understand what you meant." In such instances, there is a need to go back, to seek clarification and ensure mutual understanding.

It's tough when we don't know what we need or are scared to ask, especially when dealing with new challenges in relationships. Often, this fear comes from past trust issues. We build walls to protect our vulnerable feelings, afraid of being rejected or hurt if we show our true needs. We might think, "If I say what I want, I'll be too much," or "If I open up, I'll get abandoned."

To break down these walls and let our true selves be seen, we need to create a "safe space" in our relationships. This happens when we have clear agreements, respect each other's limits, and most importantly, communicate openly. These things help us feel secure enough to show our vulnerability, knowing it will be met with kindness, not criticism. When we have this safe space, it becomes easier to understand and express what we need, leading to deeper connections and healing old hurts.

Without clear communication, things get messy. We might hear the words but not truly understand what the other person means. That's when we need to circle back, ask questions, and make sure we're both on the same page.

In any relationship, bumps in the road are unavoidable. What matters is our ability to work through those moments with open hearts and a willingness to see each other's side. A commitment to talking things out and mending hurt feelings strengthens our safe space, allowing for more trust and closeness. When we communicate clearly, we're saying, "I see you, I hear you, I get that we're different, and I'm here for you within my own limits." Without this clear understanding and effort to fix misunderstandings, communication can get confusing and eventually break down.

Relationship ruptures are inevitable. The ability to repair any rupture through open dialogue and a willingness to understand each other's perspectives are essential for maintaining a secure and healthy connection. Revisiting misunderstandings and repairing hurt feelings reinforces the safety of the container, allowing for deeper trust and connection to flourish. In this way, we can meet the other individual based on their needs.

Through clear communication, we convey, "I see you; I hear you, I understand our differences, and within the limits of my value system, I will meet you and be there for you." Without a clear statement of needs and a commitment to addressing miscommunications and repairing any ruptures, communication can become complicated and confusing, ultimately breaking down.

Intention is the rudder of the ship; it guides all of our relationships and is a fundamental part of our core values and alignment and expression in the world.

As the journey through inner survival structures begins to resolve, something new emerges, not perfection, but wholeness. The protectors have been seen and honored. The Exiled Child has been held. The Golden Child has begun to reawaken. The Core Self, long obscured by defense and fear, now steps forward, not to dominate, but to lead with dignity, clarity, and calm.

> This is the shift:
> From reaction to response.
> From silence to truth.
> From survival to presence.

The internal system, once fragmented into avoidance, control, over-care, and panic, begins to operate as a family. A living system of parts now held by a Self, strong enough to listen without judgment, speak without fear, and choose without collapse.

And as the inner architecture finds stability, so too do our relationships. We speak more clearly. We repair more quickly. We listen without rushing to fix. We reveal without demanding to be rescued.

Because healing is not the absence of wounds, but the weaving-in of all that has been wounded. The journey of exile and return is never finished. Yet the Exile is no longer driving the system and it is no longer burdened with the impossible task of leading. Instead, it can rest, held by the Self. The child has been found. The breath has deepened. The Self is here.

A Step-by-Step Approach to Safe Relationships

1. **Establish Clear Agreements (Oaths and Mutual Rules):**
   - **Initiate Dialogue:** Begin by openly discussing the need for safety and trust in the relationship.
   - **Define Expectations:** Collaboratively identify expectations for behavior, communication, and support. What does feeling safe look like to each person?
   - **Create Explicit Agreements:** Formalize these expectations into clear, concise "oaths" or mutual rules. Examples include: "We agree to speak respectfully, even during disagreements," or "We promise to listen actively without interruption."

2. **Implement Healthy Boundaries:**
   - **Identify Limits:** Recognize and communicate individual limits regarding time, energy, emotional capacity, and personal space.
   - **Respect Boundaries:** Commit to respecting each other's boundaries without judgment or pressure.
   - **Communicate Boundary Violations:** Establish a safe way to address boundary violations when they occur.

3. **Foster Clear Communication:**
   - **Practice Active Listening:** Fully concentrate on what the other person is saying, both verbally and nonverbally. Reflect what you hear to ensure understanding.
   - **Express Needs Directly and Respectfully:** Clearly articulate your needs and feelings using "I" statements, avoiding blame or accusations.
   - **Seek Clarification:** When something is unclear, ask open-ended questions to gain a better understanding of the other person's perspective.

4. **Commit to Repairing Ruptures:**
   - **Acknowledge and Validate:** When misunderstandings or hurt feelings arise, acknowledge the rupture, and validate each other's emotions.

- **Engage in Open Dialogue:** Discuss the issue calmly and openly, seeking to understand the other person's point of view.
- **Take Responsibility:** Acknowledge your part in the rupture and apologize sincerely when appropriate.
- **Collaboratively Find Solutions:** Work together to find a resolution that addresses the concerns of both individuals.

5. **Cultivate Predictability and Trust:**
   - **Be Consistent:** Strive for consistency in your words and actions to build trust and predictability.
   - **Follow Through on Agreements:** Honor the established oaths, rules, and boundaries.
   - **Be Reliable:** Be dependable and follow through on commitments.

PRACTICE & REFLECTION:
Naming the Loss That Has No Closure

- Who in your life remains distant, physically, emotionally, or spiritually?
- What words do you wish had been spoken?
- What would change in you if you stopped waiting for them?

Write their name. Sit with it. Imagine a soft light around it. Whisper: *"I release what you cannot give. I hold what remains in grace."*

PRACTICE: SANCTUARY REHEARSAL

Find a quiet space. Sit upright, feet on the floor, spine tall. Close your eyes.

Whisper: *"I am no longer exiled. I am here now."*

Imagine the Golden Child stepping into your body like a garment made of light.

Feel what changes.

The Breath-Walker Method

When you feel triggered by a relationship, whether through criticism, abandonment, or betrayal, you can choose to walk the Breath-Walker's path.

Step 1: Recognize the Storm

Notice when your body tightens, your mind races, or old fears surge. Simply name it: "I'm triggered."

Step 2: Anchor the Body

Place your hand gently over your heart or belly. Feel the ground beneath your feet. Take three slow, deep breaths.

Step 3: Thank Your Protectors

Silently acknowledge the parts of you that want to defend or flee. Say: "Thank you. I've got this now."

Step 4: Invoke the Breath-Walker

Imagine a calm, steady presence beside you, your own Mr. Moto. Ask: "What would stillness choose here?"

Step 5: Choose a Response

From presence, not protection, choose your next step: **silence**, **distance**, a **clear boundary**, whatever honors your peace. Our healing is not a battle to win. It is a breath to return to, again and again, to live and die by our words and actions. Each time we choose presence over reaction, we honor the child within us, the one who never stopped hoping for home.

PRACTICE: AWAKENING THE GOLDEN CHILD
After calming your system with the Breath-Walker Method, invite your Golden Child to step forward. • Place a hand lightly over your heart. • Close your eyes and breathe gently. • Imagine the youngest version of yourself before shame entered the picture. • Ask softly: *"What brings you joy?"* *"What would you like to explore today?"* *"How would you dance with this moment if you were free?"* Allow whatever comes to arise without judgment. The Golden Child thrives not on perfection, but on play, wonder, and belonging. Each time you honor this spirit, you deepen your connection to the life that was always yours to live. **You were always worthy of love. You were never truly lost.**

REFLECTION: HONORING THE GOLDEN CHILD
• How does the Golden Child try to show up in your life now? • When do you feel moments of spontaneous play, trust, or wonder? • How do your protectors react to those moments, and how might the Core Self respond differently?

Breathe in. Breathe out.
Sense your surroundings, and what supports you.

HOUSE OF MIRRORS

*"In every reflection, a hidden-self calls back.
The mirrors show us what we deny, what we project,
and what we are ready to reclaim."*

— KEITH W. FIVESON

Chapter 7:
Environment, Energy, and Coherence

👣 Story: The Backyard, the Closet, and the Field of Belonging

The body knows when a space is safe, even before the mind catches up. For Willy, healing didn't end at the therapist's office or the meditation cushion. It seeped into his home, his neighborhood, the air around him. But there were places that still echoed with the past, rooms where the air felt heavier, where old memories pressed through the walls like steam.

Even in sacred spaces, the old energies can linger. Healing the home meant healing the field.

Not all healing happens in therapy, and not all integration comes from insight. Some transformations unfold quietly, in spaces where nothing seems to be happening, rooms filled with stillness, long pauses between breaths, early morning light filtered through linen curtains.

For Willy, there were specific environments where something shifted. The pace slowed. His inner system softened. The familiar vigilance gave way to a different kind of awareness. These were the spaces where something ancient and tender stirred beneath the surface.

The Golden Child would surface in those moments, brief and unspectacular to the outside world. Not as a character or a concept, but as a living presence, felt from the inside out. It would happen during meditation. In the cadence of breath. In the hush that follows a whispered prayer. It would arise in nature, in a room with soft light, in the wordless spaces of art or music. It wasn't dramatic. But it was real. The experience was less like discovering something new and more like remembering something old and sacred, a return not to a place, but to a state of being, like the space between the raindrops, or the silence beneath the sound, both near and far.

It was, in many ways, a return to the closet. Not the one filled with fear, where breath was held and sound was dangerous. The other one, the one with the secret door. The place beyond hiding. The place where Mr. Moto used to appear, not to give instructions, but simply to be. To hold space. To witness. And in this renewed version of that sacred space, another door had opened. Beauty, peace, hope, kindness, smiles, care without obligation, and presence without performance came through it authentically.

Sarah, the nurturer, found rest there. She didn't need to earn her place through over giving in this space. She was welcomed, not because she did something, but because she existed. Jason stayed near the edge, uncertain. Spaces like this felt suspicious. He had learned long ago that joy could be dangerous. Trust could be a setup. But even he didn't leave. He lingered, alert, but not running. Tom remained close and thoughtful. He appreciated the structure of silence, the rhythm of stillness. Though he didn't fully trust it yet, he respected it. He catalogued it. He stayed.

And the Golden Child? The Golden Child didn't wait at the edge. He moved freely here. He laughed, reached, rested, chanted, and sang. He belonged, not because of anything he'd done, but because this field had always been meant for him. It was his native ground. The exile had ended, not with a speech or a breakthrough, but with an environment that said, wordlessly, "You're safe here."

🌀 Teaching-Story: Environments of Becoming

In many ancient traditions, healing was never seen as separate from the environment. In Zen practice, silence, and structure hold as much power as words. The placement of stones, the rake of sand, and the breath between bells all become part of the teaching. Taoist philosophy reminds us that harmony is not achieved through striving, but by aligning with nature's rhythms. Environments, in these traditions, are not backdrops. They are participants.

Willy didn't know it then, but he had already been immersed in two radically different teachings. One was on a hippie commune in his youth, where mornings started with the smell of incense and unbrushed laughter, bodies moved freely, and names often shifting with moods. The spirit there was loose, sometimes chaotic, but undeniably juicy and alive. There were as many as thirty people, five Irish Wolfhounds, one Komondor, and a Shitsu, plus cats. He learned to share space, to listen without expectation, to live barefoot, make jewelry, and be open-hearted. The commune wasn't perfect, but it pulsed with peace, love, compassion for each other and Mother Earth. It was an ideal counterbalance to his life.

And then, there was the Army, a different type of experience. Uniforms. Precision. The sharp cut of routine. The collective breath of men rising at dawn to the bark of command. It felt akin to joining a Zen order; there was a tranquility in the discipline, a meditative rhythm in washing and cleaning, and an unwavering adherence to orders. The mess hall, where you inhaled your food, became a moment of mindful sustenance. The environment stripped away identity to build skill, discipline, and order. Every step was measured. Every bed corner is sharp. He learned to move through chaos with focus, to numb the fear and press on. This regimen taught him to obey and find peace amid the storm, a clarity from routine repetition. It wasn't nurturing, but it was formative. The Army gave him backbone. The commune gave him breath.

For Willy, one had opened the heart, and the other, the spine. The key wasn't choosing one over the other, it was learning how to hold both, to create environments that could carry freedom and form, softness, and strength.

👣 Story: Environments of Influence and Identity

And then came a different kind of environment. One not shaped by spirit or discipline, but by systems, metrics, and subtle forms of persuasion, the world of customer engagement. After the Army, Willy entered a landscape where the goal wasn't belonging, but behavior. Not healing, but influence. It began with marketing, communications, and public relations, but what he was really studying was people: how they chose, how they responded, and how environments, physical, emotional, and psychological, shaped what they believed and bought.

At first, it felt disconnected from the internal journeys he had endured. But slowly, he began to see the parallels. These were fields of influence, too, fields of meaning. Places where perception could be molded, identity could be packaged, and loyalty could be manufactured. Willy became fluent in the customer experience language, understanding how message tone, environmental cues, and demographic targeting could create a sense of trust, even intimacy. In a way, it was an architecture of the psyche. The world didn't call it spiritual, but many of the same principles applied.

He learned to orchestrate influence with precision. He saw how a product was never just a product, it was a promise. Engagement was crafted through story, rhythm, expectation, and repetition. The techniques were powerful, and Willy used them well. From brand messaging to customer journeys, from influencing purchase decisions to encouraging repeat behavior, he shaped narratives that moved people.

Tom, ever the strategist, thrived in these spaces. At a major global communications firm, he found himself among the elite, flying on corporate jets, briefing executives, guiding high-stakes presentations. He mastered the lexicon of leadership and ROI, tuned into the data that shaped decisions, and could deliver a pitch polished enough to close a multimillion-dollar deal. He was reliable, sharp, and composed. He knew how to read a room and recalibrate in real time.

But beneath his efficiency, Tom's breath was measured. His shoulders were often tight. Success came at a cost. He wasn't just managing

brands, he was working himself. Every detail had to be right. Every message had to land. Every meeting had the potential to affirm his worth or unravel it. And while others saw confidence, what lived inside was vigilance. The old training of survival had evolved, but it hadn't disappeared.

Willy watched, too. A part of him remained quietly observant, perhaps Mr. Moto, seated in the back of every boardroom, taking it all in without commentary. Because while these environments looked elegant on the surface, they often exacted a toll. They demanded performance. They commodified connection. They offered a sense of belonging, but only if you kept producing. The metrics defined the meaning. The quarterly numbers defined the value.

The Golden Child could shine in these spaces only if he dazzled. Sarah had to serve. Jason had to numb out. Tom had to control, calculate, and never lose his edge. The same protectors that had once organized around survival now reconfigured around sucwcess. But the pattern was familiar. The breath shortened. The system tightened. The exile was subtler, but no less real.

Still, something deeper remained. The lessons from the commune, the freedom, the messiness, the authenticity. The clarity from the Army, the rhythm, the structure, the inner strength. And now, a new insight from the corporate world: environments, especially those engineered for influence, mold behavior and identity. Willy began to see that the environments we build outside are often reflections of the ones we carry inside. And that true engagement, whether with a customer, a colleague, or the Self, requires coherence, not just strategy.

It would take years for Willy to integrate these lessons, but the seed had been planted. Belonging wasn't just a field to find. It was a field to create, not through manipulation or metrics, but by cultivating presence through remembering. The most powerful environments are not the ones that generate profit, they are the ones that invite us home, to return to being more conscious.

Willy saw this truth clearly, not in boardrooms, but in the spaces between them. His work and search took him across the world, through countries on nearly every continent. He sat in tea houses in Tokyo, listened to the call to prayer in Istanbul, walked barefoot through temples in Thailand, broke bread in Buenos Aires, and shared stories with shopkeepers in Ghana. Everywhere he went, the flags changed, the languages shifted, the rituals varied, but the essentials remained the same.

People wanted food that nourished them, shelter that protected them, clothes that gave them dignity, someone to love, and someone to love them

back. Whether in the high-rises of Hong Kong or the hills of Tuscany, in the deserts of the Middle East or the jungles of Central America, human needs pulsed with familiar rhythm: safety, trust, touch, and meaning.

Sometimes, these longings were hidden beneath formality or ritual. Sometimes, they were raw and visible, etched into the eyes of a refugee mother or whispered in the laughter of a child playing soccer barefoot in the street. The environments changed, but the field of belonging didn't.

It lived in gestures, in meals shared, in music carried across borders, in moments of stillness between strangers.

Willy began to understand that what he had learned through trauma, the Army, corporate life, and mindfulness was also echoed in the world's villages, cities, and sacred places: the human spirit knows how to belong when it is safe. And that field of belonging, though often covered in wounds or hardened by survival, still waits just beneath the surface, ready to rise when invited.

👣 Story: The Digital Field

There was yet another environment that Willy had helped shape, one broader, more expansive, and far more complex than any he had encountered before: the digital world. Through Tom, he had played a key role in building the infrastructure of the Internet itself. From global telecommunications to digital platforms, early machine learning (AI) and his work helped lay the groundwork for much of today's hyperconnected world. It was exciting, high-stakes work, global in scale, visionary in its reach, and driven by the promise that technology would unite people across time zones and cultures. The idea was seductive: a world where everyone could belong, instantly.

At first, it felt like that dream was real. People found their tribes. Long-lost friends reconnected. Movements formed. The world seemed smaller, more accessible, more alive with possibility. Messages traveled across oceans in seconds. The platforms he helped support became the scaffolding for a new kind of intimacy, remote work, digital friendships, instant access to information. For a time, it felt like progress.

But the deeper Willy went, the more he began to notice something else. The digital environment didn't just connect people, it reshaped the field of belonging itself. It became a space where performance often replaced presence, where profiles stood in for people, and where curated identity overtook authentic expression. At first glance, it was a vibrant landscape of connection.

But just beneath the surface, it often felt hollow, buzzing with information but starved for wisdom.

Jason, ever the avoidant protector, found comfort in numbing through endless scrolling, disappearing into the algorithmic abyss. Sarah, the nurturer, overextended herself in online communities, pouring out care in every comment thread until she felt emptied. Tom became immersed in data, metrics, and dashboards, measuring clicks, conversions, and time on-site, all in pursuit of engagement. And even the Golden Child was not immune. His voice was still present, but often filtered, edited, curated, and aestheticized. His radiance was captured in highlights but flattened by the pressure to perform.

The digital field became both a marvel and a maze. It offered intimacy without vulnerability, knowledge without integration, and attention without true attunement. Willy began to understand that the online world was not inherently evil but profoundly seductive. It invited endless stimulation while often discouraging true stillness. It created the illusion of connection while rarely inviting the kind of embodied presence that fosters real trust.

The mind scrolls faster than the soul can process. And in that dissonance, we mistake motion for meaning. True intimacy doesn't pixelate. It requires slowness. Response. Breath. And in the age of hyperconnection, disconnection often wears a beautiful filter.

Still, he couldn't reject it entirely. He had helped build it. He lived within it. But he had come to see: the digital world was not the *field*, and certainly not the place of true belonging. It was a mirror, a projection, a tool. It echoed the hunger of humanity, for connection, for meaning, for something real.

When met with presence, breath, and boundaries, it could point toward connection. But when entered unconsciously, it fed the very patterns of exile it promised to soothe. It amplified the noise, the craving, the disembodiment.

Willy realized the digital world didn't cause the disconnection.
It revealed it.

And it took real courage to look into that mirror, to witness the systemic hunger and fragmentation of modern life, and still choose to show up. Not to escape into illusion, but to seek what's real. To reclaim the deeper field of presence, one breath, one boundary, one connection at a time.

Story: Jason and the Hungry Ghost

But not everyone who wandered the digital landscape was seeking connection. For some, it became a retreat space, a seductive realm of invisibility. For Jason, the digital world offered a place not to perform, but to disappear. He wasn't interested in likes or metrics. He didn't scroll for affirmation. He scrolled to sedate, to soften the noise inside, to forget for a while. Pornography became one of his preferred paths, not for the thrill, but for the numbness it provided. In that realm, he could control the narrative. He could feel something without risking rejection. No one could touch him there, and more importantly, no one could hurt him.

These digital escapes were not new. They were echoes. Years earlier, Jason had found similar shadows on the streets of 42nd Street, in the grime of old Manhattan, where theaters offered a few minutes of flickering fantasy for a quarter and a Kleenex. It wasn't pleasure he was after, it was erasure. In those dimly lit booths and hushed corridors, he could vanish. He could release what he couldn't name. There was something scandalous and sacred in those spaces, like temples of the unwanted, altars for hungry ghosts, with nowhere else to place their longing.

Now, decades later, the everywhere mobile screen replaced the peep show, but the ache was the same. The longing to disappear, to feel without being known, to need without asking, pulsed beneath the surface. The digital environment became a new 42nd Street, a theater of endless rooms, each promising relief, none offering return. Jason didn't judge himself for it, and neither did Willy. These were adaptations, not failures, strategies of survival dressed in digital clothes.

Willy watched it unfold with a quiet awareness. He knew that Jason's escapes were not about weakness, but about wounds, old, hidden ones that had never been met with warmth. These shadow environments, both online and off, weren't inherently evil. They were simply unintegrated. They were fields filled with exiled parts, hungry ghosts, all wandering without a map.

The digital world had become something more than technology. It was a mythic landscape, a place where archetypes play out behind avatars and usernames, where longing is both inflamed and masked. It gave voice to the hidden, but often without resolution. It mimicked intimacy while avoiding vulnerability. It gave access without touch, speed without digestion, stimulation without grounding. It was not home, but it could feel like it for a moment, especially to the parts that had never truly known one.

Ultimately, Willy came to see those digital environments, like all environments, were not the issue. It was the state of the Self that entered them. When Jason entered from a place of fragmentation, the environment mirrored and multiplied this. When entered with awareness, with presence, there was room for discernment, for choice. The danger was not in the internet or the applications that support it, but in losing the thread back home to Self.

But even mirrors, even insight, are not enough on their own. What the exiled parts needed wasn't more data or distraction, it was the return to something far more ancient. A deeper field. One that could hold the shame, the numbness, the ache for contact. It wasn't the field of performance or persuasion. It wasn't the field of strategy or seduction. It was the Mother Field.

Willy began to sense it stirring beyond the noise: the field of love, compassion, and forgiveness. The place where the wounded child could be held without having to do anything. The place where Sarah could rest without serving. Where Jason could be vulnerable without disappearing. Where Tom could let go of control and simply breathe. And where the Golden Child could be welcomed home, not as a filtered version of himself, but as he truly was, radiant, raw, and honest.

This was not just a psychological return; it was sacred, cellular, a return to the field of origin, the source of safety, the womb of becoming. And perhaps, in this return, the exile would finally begin to soften, not through effort but through embrace.

Story: The Mother Field

But to truly enter the Mother Field, Willy knew he couldn't just reimagine it; he had to confront its absence. He had to walk back and look at who she was as a woman, not the perfect mother he wished for, but as the wounded woman she was. To do that meant sitting with the truth of her life, her smile, her suffering, her patterns, and her pain.

Willy remembered that she died at fifty-one, too young, and so much unresolved ache and trauma. For years, Willy had carried the weight of that loss without fully unpacking it. He knew the story on paper: alcohol poisoning, isolation, a body that had taken too much, but he had never truly stood in her shoes. Not until now. Not until he was willing to look through the eyes of compassion, to see her not as the mother who failed to protect but as the child who was never protected.

It's easy to judge from the outside, to tally mistakes, to freeze people in the moment they broke. But healing doesn't happen through blame; it occurs through witness. And when Willy began to trace her story backward, not just the end, but the beginning, he saw a lineage of loss. She was the youngest of five; two of her siblings died young. Her father drank himself to death when she was twelve. Her mother, hard, practical, emotionally scarce, did what she could, but not nearly enough. Love, in that house, was conditional. Tenderness was rare. Safety was a hope, not a given. When tenderness came from her mother's boyfriend, she responded, became pregnant, and had to give baby Kerk to her mother to care for; the boyfriend was cold and unresponsive, and she had to move on.

And so she did what many do in the wake of generational pain: she drank, she loved poorly, she gave what she could, and withheld what she didn't know how to offer. But she tried. He remembered brushing her hair, and her humming in the kitchen. Her worry, sharp and wild, when he didn't come home. Her laughter when Willy acted out television show characters. She wasn't just an alcoholic; she wasn't just the wound. She was human. And maybe, finally, that was enough.

But compassion doesn't erase pain. And bearing witness doesn't bypass the horror. At twenty-seven, Willy received the call no child should get. His mother hadn't been heard from in weeks. Neighbors complained of the smell. The police found her in her apartment, alone, her body already beginning to decompose. The coroner said it had been nearly two weeks.

Willy had to identify the body. The smell, the sight, the finality, it all carved itself into his senses. There was no poetic closure, no graceful goodbye. Death had come with silence and stench, with the cruel indifference of time and rot. And when the identification was over, the hardest part remained. He had to clean her apartment. Bag up her belongings. Scrub away the evidence of her isolation.

His brother Kerk refused to help. He harbored no love for her. To him, she had failed too profoundly, too consistently, to earn compassion. Willy didn't argue. He simply did what needed to be done. Quietly. Methodically. Room by room. With each drawer he emptied, each stained pillowcase he threw out, each photo he packed away, he wasn't just cleaning a home, he was sorting through a lineage of sorrow.

Grief didn't come in sobs. It came in waves of numbness, in the sharp metallic smell of bleach and regret. It came in the ache of a son who had loved imperfectly and been loved imperfectly in return. There was no revenge to take, no righteousness to claim. Only the slow, difficult task of telling the truth, about her, about himself, about what gets passed down and what must be laid down.

In that moment, the Mother Field was not an ideal. It was not a radiant light. It was a grave and sacred threshold. It held the terrible truth of what happens when the field is poisoned, by addiction, abandonment, and unprocessed pain. But even in that darkness, something remained. Not forgiveness, perhaps. Not yet. But the possibility of it. The wound, once witnessed, began to breathe differently. Not healed, but hallowed. In her death, she gave him no wisdom. But in her brokenness, she left him a map. A map of what not to repeat.

Standing in that empty apartment, with gloves on his hands and bile in his throat, Willy began to see her story not as a condemnation, but as a caution. A lineage that could end here. He would not run. He would not numb. He would not pass it forward. She had died in exile. He would not.

Later that night, sitting alone with the echo of that day still ringing in his chest, Sarah arrived, not with words, but with presence. She didn't ask him to process. She didn't try to make sense of what he'd seen. She simply sat beside him, barefoot, her palms open on her thighs, her eyes soft and unwavering. Her tenderness asked for nothing. It only offered space. She was the mother within, the part that knew how to love without needing to explain it. She held the grief like a warm cloth, not to erase it, but to soothe the sting.

Sarah had spent most of her life giving care reactively, cleaning up messes, diffusing tension, managing everyone else's pain before her own. But here, in this moment, she was different. She was not fixing. She was not compensating. She was simply *with him*. In her presence, the shame began to loosen. The bile in his throat softened. The part of him that had been the dutiful son, the quiet cleaner, the one who always carried the emotional weight, finally exhaled.

And then, as if the breath itself had opened a door, something shifted. The air felt different, clearer, calmer, more spacious. The tension in Willy's body began to ease. He could feel a quiet presence, not coming from outside, but rising from within.

It wasn't Sarah, as she was still there beside him, steady, calm, and caring. This was something else. Familiar. Steady. The part of him that had always watched quietly, without judgment. The Breath-Walker. The witness.

No words were spoken, but there was a sense of knowing. A message, not heard, but felt: *You're still here. Inhale. Exhale.*

This was the field, not something he had to build, but something he could return to. Beneath the grief, beneath the shame, beneath the roles and expectations. It was always there. And so was he himself empowered, individuated and alive. Willy let himself breathe again. Slowly. With Sarah's support and this quiet inner presence holding him from within. It wasn't peaceful. It wasn't resolved. But it was real. And for now, that was enough.

৩ Teaching-Story: Sacred Architecture and Design

Even though Willy's travels had taken him through more than fifty-three countries, it wasn't just the food, the people, or the landscapes that lingered, it was the sacred spaces. He began to notice how certain environments held a kind of vibrational integrity. Whether it was a temple in Kyoto, a cathedral in Rome, a Zendo in the mountains of Japan, or a quiet prayer room in a South Indian ashram, these spaces seemed to breathe. They were designed not only for function but for resonance.

In these spaces, he practiced yoga at sunrise, recited slokas under candlelight, participated in pujas that painted the air with incense and intention. He sat in stillness beneath domes that echoed breath and in rooms that seemed to magnify silence. There was something ancient and intentional about them all. The way sunlight entered. The proportions. The materials. The curves that softened thought. The geometry that aligned attention.

The ancients understood that space wasn't neutral. It could be tuned like an instrument. Cathedrals were built to echo devotion. Zen temples channeled silence with every stone path and tatami mat. The pyramids aligned with stars. Mandalas mapped the cosmos in color and symbol. Sacred geometry, based in ratios like the golden mean, reflected the underlying order of the universe, a visual echo of Shunyata's formless form.

Willy began to see that architecture could be prayer. Design could be medicine. And so, he returned home and began creating space with that reverence. A room wasn't just a room. It was a field. A container for coherence. He arranged plants not for style, but for breath. He positioned cushions not for comfort, but for openness. He tuned colors to the time of day, matched soundscapes to the light. His home became a sanctuary, not to escape the world, but to reenter it with clarity.

He was crafting his own temple, from the inside out. One that mirrored the sacred within. One that reminded him, even in chaos: the breath still flows. The space still holds.

Teaching-Story: The Inner Landscape as Environment

Willy had spent a lifetime navigating external environments, communes, battlefields, boardrooms, digital platforms, and the field of grief itself. But eventually, he came to understand that the most powerful environment was the one he carried within. The true field of belonging wasn't found in geography. It was cultivated through practice, through breath, prayer, ritual, and stillness. It was not only about creating external coherence; it was about cultivating *internal feng shui*.

The temple inside was both finite and infinite. Shaped by breath, attuned to silence, it pulsed with the potential of Shunyata, a central teaching in Mahayana Buddhism that speaks to the true nature of all phenomena: emptiness. But this emptiness is not nihilism. It is luminous potential, a fertile spaciousness from which all things arise and dissolve. Shunyata reminds us that nothing exists in isolation, that all things are interdependent, and that form and formlessness dance in every moment. Cultivating this awareness was not an abstract practice for Willy, it became a lived experience. He practiced recognizing the impermanence of thoughts, the transparency of roles, the fluidity of identity. Each breath was a letting go, each still moment a return to what was always there but never grasped.

This inner space was vast yet intimate, colored not by walls but by vibrations, intentions, and care. Plants, sacred objects, the tones of bells or chimes, a candle's flicker, these were not decorations. They were allies. Signals to the nervous system that it was time to return.

To return to breath. To air. To spirit. To the gentle wind that reminded him he was alive.

Willy learned to treat his inner space like a sanctuary. He began each day not with a to-do list, but with a breath, a deliberate, conscious inhale that stretched the chest and softened the jaw. He created altars, both literal and metaphorical, where memory and intention met. He found that sound mattered. So did light. And rhythm. The more intentional he became with the inner landscape, the more it could hold him. The more it welcomed all of his parts, Jason's guardedness, Sarah's tenderness, Tom's order, and the wild joy of the Golden Child.

This practice wasn't about perfection. It was about permission. Permission to return. Again and again. To make the internal world safe enough that no part needed to hide.

In time, he realized: the field of belonging was not just where the exile ended. It was where the return began.

Teaching-Story: Environments That Hold or Harm

Healing doesn't happen in isolation. It requires an environment that allows the nervous system to soften, the breath to deepen, and the parts to rest. Some spaces mirror old survival states, loud, disorganized, sharp around the edges. Others welcome stillness. They don't demand anything. They allow. Willy began to notice this difference, not intellectually at first, but somatically. His body would tighten in certain rooms without knowing why. His breath would shorten in certain conversations. Jason would show up at the first sign of chaos. Sarah would start tending to everyone else. Tom would scan for an exit. These reactions weren't dramatic. They were reflexive. They also taught him something essential: that the system responds to the setting.

Over time, Willy understood that the right internal or external environment is not passive. It's actively forming who we are becoming. It's shaping what parts show up and which parts go quiet. In safe, consistent, and gently structured environments, his Core Self would begin to lead. The Golden Child would linger. Mr. Moto would breathe in rhythm with the room. These environments weren't always predictable. They weren't always peaceful. But they were aligned. They had coherence. They had an intention.

Certain places became anchors. A small corner of his home, where a chair, a candle, and a few sacred objects invited him into presence. A quiet park bench.

A trusted friend's living room where listening didn't come with urgency. A spiritual community that emphasized breath over belief. In these settings, healing wasn't something to achieve. It was something that unfolded. The nervous system took the cue: you can be here, just as you are.

But not all environments supported that unfolding. Some settings activated the old defenses, the open offices, the crowded parties, the homes filled with unresolved energy and unspoken conflict. These were the spaces where exile came creeping back. The breath would be shallow. The pace would quicken. The child would retreat. The system, once again, would organize around survival.

Recognizing this pattern changed everything. Healing was not just about integrating the parts inside. It was about becoming aware of the fields outside, and choosing, whenever possible, the ones that nurtured coherence, not fragmentation.

Teaching: Somatic Belonging

Willy learned that the body, too, could become a sacred place. For trauma survivors especially, the body is often the last place they feel safe. It's where memory hides. Where numbness lives. For much of his early life, Willy had inhabited his body like a temporary visitor, functional, polite, but never quite at home.

This began to shift in unexpected places: lying still during an Ayurvedic treatment in southern India; sweating through a pranayama session in the Thai hills; holding Warrior II in a quiet Manhattan yoga studio, with breath as his only anchor. It was there, through direct experience, that Willy realized the body was not a prison, but a potential sanctuary, a holy place.

His studies deepened. He trained as a yoga teacher, exploring alignment not just of posture but of presence. He became certified in multiple massage disciplines, Shiatsu, Swedish, reflexology, and discovered how the human body responds to intentional, respectful touch. Through mindfulness practices and breath-centered movement, he slowly rewired his own nervous system. What had once felt like a battlefield became, breath by breath, a temple.

He began to learn the language of the body: **proprioception**, the sense of internal orientation; **vagal tone**, the body's ability to regulate safety and calm; the subtle cues of tension and ease. Techniques like Feldenkrais and Alexander work reminded him that every movement, how we sit, how we reach, how we hold our jaw, was a story. And those stories could be rewritten.

In his corporate life, he brought this awareness to the boardroom, learning to notice when someone's breath quickened, when a shoulder rose, when presence scattered. These weren't just signs of distraction. They were invitations to return. To pause. To ground. Somatic awareness became part of his leadership style, his coaching, his relationships.

Somatic belonging didn't come all at once. It was earned, patiently. Through discipline and permission. Through stillness and movement. Through knowing, finally, that the body, this breath, this beat, this spine, was not just a vehicle for life. It *was* life. And when met with kindness, it could become home again.

Teaching: Mapping the Field

Willy had begun to understand that belonging was not linear. It wasn't something you found once and kept, like a passport or a title. It was more like a field, alive, dynamic, and always responding to where you were and how you showed up. But one night, sitting alone with incense curling beside him and the breath soft in his chest, another image came. It was older than maps and more intimate than systems. It was Indra's Net or Web.

In this ancient Vedic metaphor, the universe is imagined as a vast net of interwoven sentient threads. At every node, a jewel rests. And in every jewel, the reflection of all other jewels is mirrored. Nothing exists alone. Each point of light contains every other. And as one shifts, so does the whole.

Willy imagined his life like that, a shimmering net of relationships, moments, sensations, memories, and spaces. Some of the jewels glowed with warmth and welcome: the kitchen where his mother once hummed, the river path where he walked after surgery, the eyes of a friend who listened without flinching. Others were cracked, distorted: the Army barracks where he numbed out, the bedroom where shame had once curled around him like smoke, the boardrooms where connection was bought and sold.

Each jewel, each connection, told a story, not just of exile or return, but of possibility. None of them were final. Even the dimmest could be polished. Even the brightest needed tending. And all were connected.

He realized that belonging wasn't about being in the right place with the right people. It was about recognizing the thread that runs through all things. The breath that moves between jewels. The silence that reflects them. The awareness that turns even wounds into light.

To map the field was not to control it. It was to witness it. To honor the brightness and the shadows. To see, perhaps for the first time, that even the places that once felt forsaken were still part of the web. Still part of the whole.

And so, the field began to settle. The parts found rhythm in the spaces he had cultivated, the breath returned without urgency, and the home became more than shelter, it became a sanctuary. The exile had not only ended within, it had ended around him.

The next chapter didn't begin with a decision. It began with a sunrise, a backyard, and the gentle knowing that he no longer had to run. He was already home.

	PRACTICE & REFLECTION: **Breath as Belonging**

Let the breath become your bridge. Use the 4–7–8 breath:
Inhale for 4.
Hold for 7.
Exhale for 8.
Repeat this cycle four times.

Then rest. Place one hand on your chest, one on your belly. Let the body soften around the breath.

REFLECT

- Which jewels glow brightly?
- Which remain dim or cracked?
- What environment would help one of these dimmed jewels shine again?

Practice: Dialogue with the Exiled Child

Find a quiet space. Let your Core Self write a short letter to the Exiled Child within you. You might begin with, *"I see you now...."* or *"I remember when you...."*

After a few minutes, switch. Let the child respond. Don't overthink. Just listen.

Reflect

- What fears or needs surfaced?
- What surprised you in the child's voice?
- What does reunion begin to feel like?

This is not about fixing. It's about presence. To listen is to begin the return.

Practice: Map Returning Home

Belonging is not a place we find, it's a space we tend. A rhythm we return to. A whisper that says, "You are not broken. You are becoming." The field you map is both ancient and alive. It reflects not only where you've been, but where you're ready to go.

These three practices invite you to pause, breathe, and gently begin that return.

Belonging is not a place we find, it's a space we tend. A rhythm we return to. A whisper that says, "You are not broken. You are becoming." The field you map is both ancient and alive. It reflects not only where you've been, but where you're ready to go.

These three practices invite you to pause, breathe, and gently begin that return.

Map Your Field

Use the *Mapping Your Field* visual as a personal constellation. In the center circle, place your Core Self. Around it, name the people, places, practices, and moments that have shaped your sense of belonging, or your experience of exile.

Some may feel warm, alive, trustworthy. Others may still sting or go quiet in your body. That's okay. This map is not a judgment. It's a witness. A field in motion.

Trace the thread between them. Notice what moves in your breath as you do

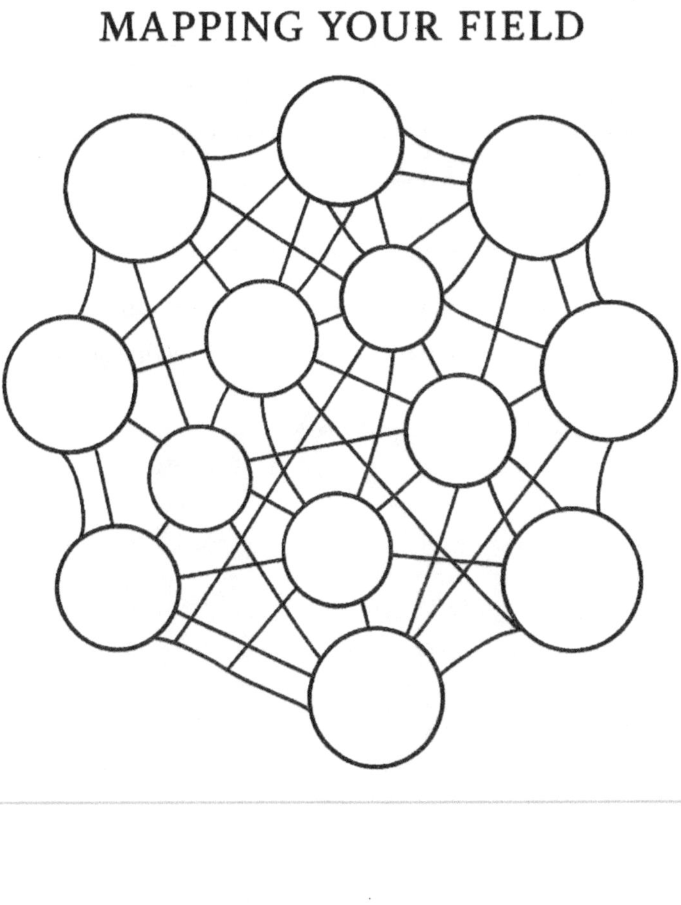

MAPPING YOUR FIELD

The Threshold Between

Before we arrive home, we pause at the doorway.

You've breathed. You've remembered. You've listened to the whispers of the Exiled Child, maybe even answered them. You've softened around the places that once held only tension. Something has begun to shift.

Not everything is clear. Not every part is ready. That's okay.

This is the space in between.

Not the exile. Not yet the return. But the place where something opens. The moment when you don't have to keep running or hiding. You can just be.

Feel your breath again now. Let it anchor you.

If you've come this far, something in you is already turning homeward. The story is no longer just behind you, it's within you, reshaping. What you once saw as broken might now be seen as becoming.

The light is near. So is the child.

And the house is not as far away as it once seemed.

Let us begin the return.

Breathe in. Breathe Out.
Be aware of your body and surroundings.
The floor, ceiling, the walls, and your environment,

Journey Home

*"The journey home is not a return to what was lost,
it is a union with what was never truly gone."*

– Keith W. Fiveson

Chapter 8:
The Arrival Home

👣 Story: Presence After Exile

There are moments when healing isn't loud, it arrives like tidewater at sunset. After the breathwork, after the vision, Willy found himself where he hadn't expected to be: home.

It was summer on the bay of the Long Island Sound. He was on the North Shore.

He was in his late 60's and he wasn't running anymore. . . . He had arrived.

Summer on Long Island Sound, the "Gold Coast," a year after heart surgery, a lifetime after exile. Willy sat in the backyard, bare feet on warm slate stone, listening to the slow rhythm of waves in the distance and cicadas in the

trees. He wasn't running anymore. Not from shame. Not from longing. Not from himself.

He had food, shelter, clothing. People he loved, and who, miraculously, loved him back. The old ache to belong had softened. For the first time in decades, he wasn't searching for a place to land. He was home. . . .

Ten miles southwest, on the South Shore, lay the town where the closet still stood, the one with mothballs, leather shoes, and the ghost of a three-year-old boy. But that place no longer held him captive. The past hadn't vanished. It had simply found its place.

The warm late-day sun filtered through the trees. The salt air of the bay clung to his skin. A breeze lifted a wind chime overhead. It sounded like a distant lullaby. He closed his eyes. And there they were.

Willy, the child, barefoot and blinking in the fading sun. Jason, the armor, upright but softened. Tom, the strategist, contemplative. Sarah, the caregiver, her hands open on her lap. Mr. Moto, the witness, quiet as breath. All seated beside him in silence, not as fragments, but as family.

For so long, each had taken turns steering the ship, trying to survive. Now, none needed to lead. They were no longer exiled from each other. They were home. Whole.

And in the quiet, another presence stirred, not in the mind, not in the body, but in the space between. The Golden Child. Luminous. Centered. Unafraid.

"You made it," he seemed to whisper, though no words were spoken. "You brought us all home."

Willy smiled. Not because he had conquered anything, but because he had stopped fighting.

This was Dharma, not a role to play, but a rhythm to live by. Not perfection, but presence. Not answers, but alignment. Dharma isn't a job title, a role, or a performance. It's the quiet alignment between breath, purpose, and presence.

The backyard creaked as he leaned back in his chair. His breath was slow and even. His heart, newly mended, pulsed with gratitude.

He wasn't just surviving anymore.
He was living.
He was here.
He was whole.

But arriving home wasn't the beginning. It was what came after the storm.

Before the Backyard

He had not always lived this way.

There was a time, decades even, when Willy's life was more storm than sanctuary. Before the plants and prayer flags, there were sterile apartments, empty bottles, and long nights filled with noise. Before Morocco, Kerala, and Rajasthan, there were hotel rooms, boardrooms, and backrooms, each a stage for a man trying to outrun the echo of his own name.

In his twenties, he was already a survivor of family ruptures, secrets buried in closets, and betrayals too tangled to explain. He joined the Army not for patriotism but for structure. It gave him a spine when all he had was pain. But when the uniform came off, the ache returned, polished now, but no less sharp.

He built a career, even an empire of sorts, in communications. He learned how to sell trust without needing to feel it. He could move markets, shape perceptions, and influence outcomes. But behind every confident handshake and closed deal was a man who couldn't sleep through the night. Two marriages fell apart. Each time, he told himself it was the job, the pressure, the timing. But the truth was harder: he didn't know how to stay.

In those years, travel became his therapy: hundreds of flights, thousands of photos. From Japanese temples to Colombian coastlines, he chased awe like a man dying of thirst. And in some ways, he was. He collected masks, textiles, incense holders, objects that offered beauty, even when he couldn't yet offer it to himself.

The turning point didn't come all at once. It came in chapters, slow, faltering, unfinished. A Taoist yoga retreat in Thailand. A friend's overdose. A glimpse of his reflection after too many years of looking away. The two cancers, then the heart surgery, open, invasive, humbling. Lying in the ICU, tubes in his chest, machines monitoring his breath, he met something ancient inside himself: silence.

That was the beginning, not of something new, but of something whole. A man in the backyard, surrounded by relics of culture and spirit, who wasn't born yesterday. He was excavated, layer by layer, scar by scar. And now, he sits not as a man without pain, but as a man no longer ruled by it. A well-decorated home with sacred objects gathered from over five decades of travel held soul, story, and reverent presence. Willy no longer sought transcendence in temples or rituals alone. His life had become the temple. The food on his table, the texture of cloth against his skin, and the breath shared with those he loved

were sacraments. Each item, from handwoven rugs to prayer flags, wooden carved sacred statues, and adornments, carried a personality, a resonance, an energy that reflected the depth of the journey.

Live palm trees, thriving plants, soft lighting, and bespoke furniture from places like Sri Lanka, Rajasthan, and Morocco filled the rooms with warmth and beauty. Like Willy's heart, the home had become a temple, a curated ecosystem of presence and memory. He now saw his days imbued with sacred meanings and layered blessings.

Willy's deepest transformation wasn't forged in solitude, it was reflected, challenged, and deepened through relationship. At the center of this evolution was the woman he married, for her sense of compassion, justice, humor, admiration, and truth. A lover, friend, and companion for over three decades, a strong, emotionally intelligent woman who neither tolerated his defenses nor colluded with his fears. She was fiercely autonomous, spiritually grounded, and deeply compassionate, but not passive. She demanded presence. She called him forward. One evening, after a difficult silence, she reached across the table, not with words, but with a glance that said, "I see you." He didn't flinch. That was new.

Unlike previous partners who reinforced his patterns of escape or self-neglect, his wife offered a mirror he couldn't ignore. When Willy attempted to avoid or outmaneuver intimacy, she held her ground. When he tried to rationalize his way out of vulnerability, she remained rooted in emotional truth. With her, he learned that real love was not about merging or fixing, but witnessing, respecting, and evolving together.

Their marriage became not just a bond, but a practice, a Dharma of relationship. Through her unwavering authenticity, his wife challenged Willy to dismantle his survival strategies. She invited his Exiled Child to step out of the closet, his Strategist to take a breath, his Caregiver to receive for once. She made it safe to be real. And in doing so, she became both a true companion and catalyst.

In the space between them grew the fertile ground of transformation. Through illness, joy, loss, travel, stillness, and silence, they weathered life as co-journeyers, each committed to truth. Their love became a sanctuary, not of perfection, but of mutual accountability and sacred disruption.

The presence of his grandchildren in his life made him happy. Grandkids were three minutes to four hours away, and visits were as frequent as possible. These gatherings transformed ordinary moments into sacred rituals

of continuity, joy, and healing. For Willy, these golden years are a return to domestic peace, and a profound reentry, through suffering, silence, and breath, into a state of embodied wholeness he once thought unreachable. In the echo of his grandchildren's laughter, something stirred, not just memory, but a presence, the Golden Child. Not a ghost of innocence lost, but a living, breathing part of him, awake and playful again.

With time, Willy became increasingly selective about the frequencies he allowed into his space, which included family and friends. People, places, and objects should have a positive resonance, energetic, emotional, spiritual, and life-giving. Willy distanced himself from people and environments steeped in drama or dissonance. Solitude was no longer something to be avoided but cherished as a sanctuary. He became more comfortable with his company than with rocky relationships. Presence, he understood, did not require an audience. It only needed authenticity.

He practiced each morning with meditation at 5 a.m., centering himself in breath, stillness, and gratitude. Throughout the day, he brought conscious awareness to each moment, chewing every bite slowly, clearing his palate, and moving deliberately through his environment. This wasn't just mindfulness as practice; it was mindfulness as lifestyle. He chilled, laughed, and allowed himself to be. He focused on his recovery and devoted time to supporting a small group of carefully chosen clients. Plant medicine became a deepening part of his inner work again, particularly in contexts of death, dying, and renewal. His reentry into the plant medicine community was thoughtful, grounded, and guided by intention. Willy now embodied healing not as a destination but as a way of life, rooted in breath, choice, and reverent participation with the present. Once the inner architecture was strong enough to hold presence, he began offering it to others.

Willy began volunteering with the Heroic Hearts Project, an organization dedicated to helping veterans access healing through psychedelic-assisted therapy. As a veteran himself, and a survivor of exile, addiction, and early trauma, Willy recognized the depth of suffering many of these men carried, unseen, misdiagnosed, or buried beneath layers of stoicism. He brought to his work with them not just his professional experience, but his scars. And those mattered more.

He served as a healthcare ambassador and advocate, helping to raise awareness about the potential of plant medicine and psychedelic-assisted therapies for trauma recovery. His role wasn't to guide individual journeys directly, but to educate, share his own story, and help destigmatize these approaches among veterans and their families. He spoke at community events, contributed to outreach efforts, and worked to expand access to these therapies within safe, structured containers that emphasized preparation, integration, and informed choice.

In his private coaching and small group circles, Willy supported men exploring the intersection of trauma, masculinity, and transformation. He didn't position himself as an expert with all the answers. Instead, he offered space, space to be broken, to be honest, to be held. Through story work, breath practices, and archetypal reflection, he helped men name the parts of themselves that longed for belonging and identify where they had drifted out of alignment.

Some showed up armored like Jason, emotionally distant and skeptical of vulnerability. Others strategized like Tom, trying to think their way out of pain. A few gave everything to everyone, like Sarah, exhausted and invisible in their own lives. Willy recognized these patterns immediately. He had lived them. Sat in silence with them. Breathed them home.

Most profoundly, he witnessed men reconnect with their own Golden Child, the sacred essence of who they were before the trauma, before the uniform, before the exile. In those moments, he wasn't a healer but a mirror, reflecting back the possibility of wholeness.

This work wasn't a pivot, it was a continuation. His history had become medicine. What once fueled escape now guided return. The same parts that chased success, numbed pain, or micromanaged his world now served as trusted allies in helping others remember who they were.

In every man he sat with, he saw some version of himself. And in every healed moment, he knew: this was his Dharma. Not a job. Not a role. But a rhythm. A remembering. A way of walking in the world with reverence for the pain, and joy in the possibility of return.

꧁ Teaching-Story: Integration

From a clinical perspective, Willy's journey reflects the arc of post-traumatic growth within a framework that integrates Internal Family Systems (IFS), mindfulness-based practices, and the principles of narrative and aspirational living. His early years had been shaped by exile, familial neglect, disconnection, and the suppression of his Authentic Self. These early patterns manifested in adult life through two failed marriages and an overreliance on cognitive defenses, particularly the managerial strategies of Tom, his internal rational protector. In IFS terms, the Golden Child wasn't just an archetype. He was the unburdened essence of Willy's exile, creative, joyful, spontaneous. The Self didn't just lead; it danced.

In his later years, Willy pursued advanced training through the Integrative Psychiatry Institute, deepening his understanding of trauma, neurobiology, and the interface between psychedelics, psychotherapy, and spiritual integration. His deepening engagement with plant medicine was not merely personal but vocational. He recognized the enormous potential these substances held for addressing complex trauma, PTSD, and behavioral use disorders, especially in those whose nervous systems had long been organized around survival.

His own experiences with psycholytic cannabis and ketamine therapy allowed him to witness firsthand the power of quieting the Default Mode Network (DMN), loosening the grip of ruminative thought patterns, and creating enough space for the exiled parts of the psyche to be seen and held.

Willy began supporting other veterans and clients who were considering or engaging in psychedelic-assisted therapy, not by administering or guiding sessions himself, but by providing education, preparation, and integration support. He helped individuals explore intentions, develop mindfulness skills to navigate altered states, and reflect on their experiences afterward to foster meaning and coherence.

These weren't recreational escapes but part of a continuum of healing. Willy brought the same grounded presence he had cultivated through decades of personal work to these conversations. He became a steward of readiness and return, helping others move from fragmentation toward wholeness, not through administering medicine, but through conscious preparation, compassionate witnessing, and integration of the insights that emerged.

The same protector parts that once drove him toward performance and perfection now supported his mission to care, witness, and hold others as they

confronted their shadows. His history, of exile, addiction, and self-repair, became the soil from which authentic service grew. He applied this training in his professional work, coaching men in recovery. His focus was on helping clients rebuild trust in themselves and their internal systems after long-standing patterns of addiction and alienation. His coaching practice became a mirror of his growth, rooted in mindful presence, informed by evidence-based modalities, and delivered with heart-forward compassion.

Through years of practice, Willy learned to recognize and unburden his protective parts, stepping back from their grip and allowing their deeper wisdom to emerge. Jason, once the armored survivor, softened into stability and trust in the presence of loved ones. Tom, the relentless strategist, eased his need for control, making space for intuition, spontaneity, and joy. Sarah, the tireless caregiver, discovered the gift of rest and quiet, learning that her worth was not measured by constant doing or caretaking. Each part, once burdened, found a healthier role within Willy's inner family.

Through it all, Mr. Moto, the Self, the Breath-Walker, offered a steady guide, appearing in moments of stillness, especially during contemplative practice and ceremony. Yet beyond simply witnessing, another presence began to take shape, the Golden Child. No longer just a flicker or a forgotten archetype, the Golden Child emerged as the embodied integration of all the parts: playful, alive, authentic, and whole.

This emergence was not just symbolic, it was cellular. With every breath, Willy experienced what it meant to be fully alive, to recognize both the pain and the blessings, and to celebrate joy without guilt. The Golden Child was not a fantasy; he was the embodied outcome of healing, the evidence that wholeness was not only possible but already unfolding.

Your Golden Child still lives within you, waiting not for perfection, but for presence. You don't need to be healed to begin. You only need to start to remember who you are.

Watching his grandchildren opened a new doorway into healing. Their spontaneous play, joy, and curiosity reflected something deep within Willy, an invitation to reconnect with parts of himself long buried. In their laughter,

he saw what had been missing: the freedom to be unguarded, the safety to be seen. Sitting with them, he didn't just witness love, he felt it ripple backward in time. At ages three, fourteen, or eighteen, they mirrored the child he once was and the man he had become. These moments didn't erase his past, but softened it, filling old cracks with warmth and possibility. In these simple, shared connections, Willy experienced what therapy alone could not offer, a living sense of wholeness, held across generations.

In writing a reflective letter to his younger self, age nineteen, post-trauma, pre-Army, Willy articulated a form of compassionate reparenting. The letter served both as a narrative intervention and a corrective emotional experience. By acknowledging his suffering while offering a future-oriented vision of resilience, Willy closed a critical loop in his trauma narrative. In one section, he wrote:

"You're going to be alright, Willy. Life is going to get better and better. The pain you feel now will shape your strength. The losses will deepen your empathy. One day, these will be the 'good old days', not because they were easy, but because they were real. We'll get through this, and one day, we'll sit together again, not in pain, but in peace."

This gesture of inner reconciliation marked the culmination of years of therapeutic work, where self-compassion replaced self-judgment and the exile of the past was invited into the heart of the present.

This moment signals the final movement in Willy's Hero's Journey, not merely a return, but a sacred reintegration. He did not emerge from exile with trophies, but with tenderness. The battle was never to win something outside himself, but to become fully present to all that lived within. Wholeness was no longer a concept, it had become embodied. And so this became a natural pause in the narrative, where we transition from the arc of becoming to the field of belonging, not as a destination, but as a daily practice.

Though shaped by complexity and loss, his life had become a living embodiment of presence. He now prioritized coherence over performance, connection over control. And as he sat, body grounded, breath steady, surrounded by the echoes of laughter, he embodied a truth well known in contemplative traditions: that home is not a place we find but a presence we cultivate.

Yet this was not the end of his journey. Rather, it became a threshold for others. As the narrative deepens, we invite readers to take stock of their own inner and outer landscapes through the tools of Internal Family Systems (IFS), archetypal reflection, and the Monomythic arc of the Hero's Journey. Willy's

path opens the door for others to do the same: to name their parts, trace their exiles, recognize their protectors, and begin building their own bridges home. You are not broken. You are becoming. The exile is over. Welcome home.

In the following pages, we move from story to structure, offering exercises, maps, and reflections for those ready to embark on their journey of becoming whole. Because belonging is not inherited, it's cultivated. And healing, while personal, is never private. It touches all those we meet, across generations, across time.

Archetypal Self-Inquiry: Who Walks with You?

Objective: Explore the survival and aspirational archetypes that guide and shape your inner world.

The Return of the Golden Child: A Reflection on Wholeness

The return isn't about becoming someone new. It's about remembering who you've always been.

As you've moved through these pages, through wounds, archetypes, masks, and moments of tenderness, you've also been circling closer to your essence. Not a perfect Self. Not a finished Self. But a *True Self.*

The Golden Child is not a fantasy or a distant memory. It is a living energy, an aspect of your being that holds joy, wonder, wisdom, and the capacity to love. It may have been buried, silenced, or distorted, but it was never lost.

This final reflection invites you to pause and notice what has returned, what is still returning, and what it means to live a life where the Exiled Child is no longer alone.

Practice & Reflection:
Write Your Return: A Self-Authorship Exercise

1. **The Story I've Been Living . . .**

   "What narratives about myself have shaped the way I live, love, protect, or hide?"

2. **The Parts I've Met Along the Way . . .**

   "Which inner archetypes or protective roles have shown up in my life?"
   - Who guarded me?
   - Who got exiled?
   - Who still needs to be welcomed home?

3. **The Call I'm Hearing Now . . .**

   "If my life is a Hero's Journey, what threshold am I standing on now?"

4. **My Golden Child Knows . . .**

   "What does my joyful, spontaneous Self, love, create, and long for?"

5. **A Letter to Myself (Optional):**

   "Write a one-page letter from your current Self to the child or younger version of you, as Willy did."

6. **Author Your Next Chapter:**

   "Title the next chapter of your life, and write a short paragraph about the values and presence you want it to carry."

Narrative Practice: A Letter to the Exiled Child

Write a letter to your younger, exiled self. Let this letter come not from a place of fixing or analyzing, but from **Presence**.

You might begin with:

*"I see you now. I remember you. And I want you to know:
I'm here. You're not alone anymore."*

You can let this letter be gentle or fierce, brief, or poetic. Let it be real. This is a sacred reunion, not the end of your story, but the beginning of wholeness.

> **INTEGRATION REFLECTION:**
> **The Return of the Golden Child: Calm. Curiosity. Compassion.**
> **Confidence. Clarity. Courage. Creativity. Connectedness.**
>
> 1. Which parts of you have softened, come into awareness, or begun to trust since beginning this journey?
> 2. Which of the 8 C's of the True Self feel most alive in you now?
> 3. What does the Golden Child within you want to say or do today?
> 4. If you could create a safe space in your life where that part of you could play, speak, rest, or lead, what would it look like?
> 5. What does wholeness mean to you now? Has your definition changed?

You have arrived home. You are not broken.

You are becoming. The exile is over. Welcome home.

Not the end.

Just the breath between chapters.

Chapter 9:
The Path Forward

👣 Story: A Rhythm-Not a Race

If you've come this far, pause. Breathe. Recognize the courage it takes to face your inner terrain, the exile, the fragmentation, the return. You've met parts of one man's story, Willy, Jason, Tom, Sarah, Mr. Moto, and perhaps, somewhere along the way, glimpsed echoes of your own. These weren't just characters. They were maps, mirrors, and invitations to explore the landscape of your own becoming. These archetypes weren't characters for entertainment. They were carriers of memory, emotion, and survival. They were invitations to explore your own internal constellation.

Now, as we turn toward the end of this book, we also turn toward a new beginning, not the end of healing, but the start of a deeper practice of living. Healing is not a finish line. It's a rhythm. A way of being. A path that requires us to show up each day with awareness, compassion, and humility.

Our culture often teaches us to pursue growth as a linear journey: you begin broken, work hard, and arrive at some perfected version of yourself. But in truth, healing is a spiral. You return again and again to the same core themes, belonging, safety, love, truth, but each time with a little more awareness, a little more capacity to be with what is. You don't become a new person. You remember who you've always been beneath the layers of conditioning and defense.

That's why the work of integration is ongoing. You might feel clear and whole one day, only to feel shaken or thrown off the next. This doesn't mean you've failed. It means you're alive. Growth does not protect us from life's difficulties. What it offers is a different way of relating to them, with less judgment and more presence.

You don't need grand gestures. Your life, exactly as it is, offers daily invitations to return. The way you greet yourself in the mirror before brushing your teeth. The moment you pause before snapping at your partner. The choice to sit

with a morning coffee without reaching for your phone. The way you respond to discomfort, the quality of attention you bring to a conversation, or a moment of silence, these are sacred. Healing happens not only in therapy rooms or ceremonies, but in kitchens, hallways, coffee shops, and quiet moments with yourself. This is what I mean when I say your life is the ceremony.

You are not required to become someone new. You are invited to become more yourself. The child within you, the one who once held wonder, curiosity, and play, has not disappeared. They've been waiting, watching, hoping you'd return. That Golden Child is not an ideal to achieve, but an essence to reclaim. They don't ask for perfection. They ask for presence.

As you continue your journey, consider the practices that ground you, not out of obligation, but out of love. Create space for reflection in the morning. Name the parts that show up when you feel reactive or closed off. Practice breathing through the tension rather than pushing it away. Surround yourself with people and places that nourish your nervous system and your soul. When you fall back into old patterns, and you will, practice returning without shame. That is the rhythm of this work.

Community matters too. Though healing often begins in solitude, it deepens in relationship. Find others who are also learning to return to themselves. Speak your truth. Listen without fixing. Let yourself be witnessed and let yourself witness others. When we come home to ourselves, we create space for others to do the same.

As you walk forward, remember that you are the steward of your own integration. No outside authority can walk this path for you. But you are not alone. Others are walking beside you, quietly and courageously, in their own ways. Every step you take ripples outward, touching those around you: friends, children, clients, even strangers.

Let this final chapter be less of an ending and more of a pause. A breath. A quiet place to gather yourself before continuing on. The tools you've explored, IFS, breath, story, archetype, mindfulness, are not final answers. They are invitations to stay engaged, to keep listening, and to remain curious.

You don't have to have it all figured out. You only need to keep choosing presence over perfection. You only need to keep choosing return.

Let this be your rhythm. Not a race, but a way of living, with reverence for the pain and joy in the possibility of becoming whole.

Breathe first.
Inhale: remember.
Exhale: return.
Name the part.
Stay present.
Return without shame.
Let wholeness be the work.

Reflection: Author's Wish

Though much of this story was told in the third person, the journey has always been personal. Willy is not just a character, he is the echo of my own Exiled Child, the voice I once silenced, the boy who kept breathing even when he didn't know how to belong.

Each archetype, Jason, Tom, Sarah, Mr. Moto, and the Golden Child, represents a part of my own inner constellation. I've lived their patterns. I've worn their masks. And over time, I've learned to sit with them, to hear their wisdom, and to welcome them home.

This book is an ancient memory, a medicine bundle, weaving narrative, trauma, healing, Internal Family Systems, and mindfulness. My hope is that through these pages, you not only witnessed a return, but felt a stirring of your own. A remembering.

You may not have had the same story, but perhaps you've felt the same exile. If so, I want you to know this: you are not broken. You are becoming. And the path back isn't linear, it's breath by breath, scar by scar, choice by choice.

The Golden Child still lives within you, not waiting for perfection, just for presence.

Thank you for walking this far with me. May you continue your own return, with courage, compassion, and love.

If we ever meet in person, I'll recognize you, not by your face, but by your breath. The way you carry your story. The way you return to who you've always been.

Afterword: Author's Note

This book carries not only wisdom but wounds. If you listen closely, you may hear the echoes of my own shadows between these pages, along with the hunger I once hid, the silences I could not break, the scars that I still remember. They are not mistakes. They are threads of the same fabric that holds the light.

I release this work knowing it may be misunderstood. Some will find in it a mirror, others a question, and still others may set it aside. That is as it should be. Once written, a book is no longer mine to keep, since it now belongs to you, the reader, to carry, to question, to reshape.

This is not memoir alone, nor is it a manual. It is both. It is a map stitched from lived experience, from teachings and traditions that guided me, and from the clinical and contemplative practices that gave language to what I could not say as a child. It stands at the threshold between personal and collective, between story and study, between what I lived and what I continue to learn.

If anything endures beyond these words, may it be this: that even in exile, you are not broken. That the child within you waits, not for perfection, but for presence. And that returning home is never too late because home is not a place, but the heartbeat you carry.

Acknowledgments

First and foremost, my deepest thanks go to my beloved wife, Charlotte. She has been my lighthouse for over thirty years-illuminating truth, calling me to courage, and grounding me with love. Her wisdom and unwavering support have been vital to my journey of healing and self-reclamation.

To our blended family, Justin, Michael, and Scottie, and to our seven grandchildren, Gunnar, Damian, Eliza, Robbie, Lily, Allie, and R.J.: you are my heart. Your presence in my life has given me the opportunity to rewrite the past through new expressions of love. Through you, I have found purpose, humility, and joy.

To the countless clients, friends, teachers, and fellow seekers: you have each played a role in helping me remember who I am. While names and stories have been changed throughout these pages, your courage is deeply etched into the soul of this work. Thank you for sharing your humanity and trusting me with yours.

To the mentors and communities who shaped my understanding, teachers of Internal Family Systems, mindfulness, and contemplative practice, and to the Heroic Hearts Project, whose ongoing work with veterans struggling with PTSD and trauma is close to my heart and continues to inspire me: I am grateful for your wisdom and example.

Throughout this book, you may have noticed multiple shifts in voice, from the immediacy of first person to the reflective distance of third person. This was a deliberate choice, weaving together Story, Teaching, Practice, and Reflection. Sometimes we need to step outside our own story to witness it with compassion, almost as if sitting beside the younger self we once left behind. Other times, we must speak directly from the center of memory. This is not fiction; it is the way I have learned to hold experience with curiosity and care.

Finally, to those who challenged me, through betrayal, misunderstanding, or mindlessness, it is you who have most sharpened my resolve. To the reader who dared to turn these pages: may you discover that your Exiled Child has always been waiting for you to come home. May your return be gentle, kind, and true.

Selected References & Suggested Readings

- Campbell, J. (1949). *The Hero with a Thousand Faces.* Princeton University Press.
- Epston, D., & White, M. (1990). *Narrative Means to Therapeutic Ends.* Norton.
- Grof, S. (2001). *Psychology of the Future: Lessons from Modern Consciousness Research.* State University of New York Press.
- Grof, S. (1988). *The Adventure of Self-Discovery.* SUNY Press.
- Jung, C. G. (1968). *Archetypes and the Collective Unconscious.* Princeton University Press.
- Kabat-Zinn, J. (1990). *Full Catastrophe Living: Using the Wisdom of Your Body and Mind to Face Stress, Pain, and Illness.* Delta.
- Lao Tzu. *Tao Te Ching.* (Multiple translations, e.g., Stephen Mitchell, 1988, Harper & Row).
- Schwartz, R. (1995). *Internal Family Systems Therapy.* Guilford Press.
- White, M. (2007). *Maps of Narrative Practice.* Norton.
- Wilber, K. (2000). *Integral Psychology: Consciousness, Spirit, Psychology, Therapy.* Shambhala.

Epilogue: The Quiet Return

The journey you have just walked through these pages is not only mine. It is the journey of all of us who have ever felt exiled from our own hearts, who have learned to survive by hiding, pleasing, performing, or running.

If there is one truth I hope you carry, it is this: you were never truly lost. Even in the darkest seasons, something in you, some small, steady ember, was waiting. Waiting for you to turn toward it, to remember who you were before the world taught you to forget.

This is the work of returning:
To feel what was once unbearable.
To honor the protectors that kept you alive.
To welcome the Exiled Child with compassion instead of shame.
To let the Golden Child step forward, not as a fantasy but as your birthright.

No guide, book, or teacher can do this work for you. But you are not alone. Every time you pause to breathe, every time you meet yourself with gentleness, you are part of a larger field of belonging that holds us all.

May you trust your own timing. May you honor your own pace. May you know that there is no perfect offering, only the willingness to keep showing up, imperfect and whole.

And when you doubt, as we all do, remember the crack that lets the light in. Remember that the exile ends not with triumph, but with a breath and a quiet return.

You belong. You always have. You always will.

Warm Regards,

Keith

This book is a gift, and it carries Keith's heart on every page.

Sabina Erlich – *Psychotherapist & Dharma*

It takes tremendous courage to share one's deepest pain with the world in the hope of illuminating a path of healing for others. The writing and publication of this book is a true act of bodhisattva activity.

Jacqueline Van Den Bovenkamp – *Artist & Mindfulness Practitioner*

I was grabbed by the book from the start. The story of Willy is compelling, and the blend of Jung, Taoism, and IFS wisdom makes the narrative both profound and accessible.

Catherine Maudsley (Short Form) – *Art Historian & Educator*

In this searingly honest account, Keith W. Fiveson takes us on a personal journey framed by IFS and other healing systems, offering reflections and somatic practices for genuine personal growth.

Chris Caldwell – *End-of-Life Partnerships*

Through his deeply personal stories, Keith displays a gift for taking all of us on our own journey to wholeness. His superpower is helping us see the parts of ourselves buried deep and bringing them to light and love. *This is not a book to be read and tucked away; it is to be lived each day.*

Kim Andrews – *Educator & Writer*

Return of the Exiled Child is like having a personal therapist in your pocket. Each section invites practice and reflection through prompts and breathwork – a companion for anyone ready to face their own healing journey.

Zubin Kapadia – *Advocate for Aging with Dignity | Home Care & Healthcare Expert | Entrepreneur | Champion for Education & Workforce Development*

I've known Keith Fiveson for more than 25 years, and even with all the conversations and life chapters we've shared, *Return of the Exiled Child* opened a window into his journey that moved me deeply.

Keith invites readers into the most vulnerable parts of his life — childhood trauma, loss, illness, and the long path back to wholeness — and he does it with honesty, courage, and clarity that only someone who has truly done the inner work can offer.

His integration of mindfulness, IFS, breath, and spiritual wisdom doesn't feel theoretical; it feels lived, embodied, and hard-earned.

What I love most is that the book reflects the Keith I know: grounded, compassionate, and always searching for truth. This isn't just a memoir - it's a guide for anyone trying to reconnect with the parts of themselves they've hidden or forgotten.

www.ingramcontent.com/pod-product-compliance
Lightning Source LLC
LaVergne TN
LVHW041638060526
838200LV00040B/1614